Celebration of Life

The Story of Life Care Centers of America

Photography by Robin Hood
Text by Barry Parker

PARKER HOOD
PRESS

mation, contact: Office of the Executive Vice President for Corporate and
ity Relations, Life Care Centers of America, Inc., 3570 Keith Street,
, TN 37312, phone: 423/472-9585; or: Parker Hood Press, Inc., 340 Crest
rive, Chattanooga, TN 37404; phone: 800/563-1235

Congress Control Number: 00-091031

545704-5-9

by Robertson Design, Inc., Brentwood, Tennessee
s by Color Systems, Inc., Nashville, Tennessee
China through Asia Pacific Offset, Inc.
by Parker Hood Press, Inc., Chattanooga, Tennessee

TION

To the residents of our centers, who enrich our lives,

and to the associates, who care for our residents with respect and affection,

we dedicate this book.

Celebration of Life

The Story of Life Care Centers of America

Dear Dr. Miller:

It has been my privilege to get to know you. You have been a great example of Service and Compassion. I will always remember with great fondness in occasions of reflections about our times together. May God bless you!

— Beecher Hunter
17 May 06

Introduction

She *was a woman of grace and beauty,* endowed with a charm that drew others to her. And if you were around Dorothy Giehm long, your laughter had a little more lilt to it and your step had a bit more spring in it.

She had a love affair with life, you see, and her ardor for it enveloped those who came near her. She pursued the relationship — this courtship with time — passionately and with determination. As a result, the fruits of peace, joy, happiness and fulfillment abounded within her soul.

Mrs. Giehm's wonderful journey through three centuries — consider that amazing statement — came to an end on February 4, 2000, at Life Care Center of Tucson in Arizona, where she was a resident at the place she proudly called her home.

Less than one month before, on January 10, Mrs. Giehm celebrated her 108th birthday anniversary, surrounded by family and friends. It was a remarkable and memorable occasion, with gifts, hugs aplenty, refreshments and lots of laughter.

The tenderest and most poignant moments of the party, however, involved only two people, even though there were 40 or more in the room. On several occasions — whether at the presentation of a gift, the touching of hands, an embrace or a look of admiration — Dorothy Giehm, the resident, and Forrest Preston, the nursing home owner, seemed frozen in space and time, alone together on an island in a small sea of humanity.

The affection between them was deep and genuine, formed when they met at a luncheon in the center five years earlier. A catalyst for their friendship was her gregarious nature in general and her mirth in particular. "You couldn't be in her presence without the laughter," Preston said. "It was the same magic that captivated me when she was but 103 years old and adopted me as her nephew. It was the same enchantment that she cast over our entire management meeting when she came to Cleveland, Tennessee, in 1998, at 106."

To Preston, and all of his Life Care associates at the 1998 gathering, Dorothy Giehm was an icon for what Life Care Centers of America is all about.

Even though it is a business, with issues of management contracts, mortgages, accounts payable and receivable, census, demographics and turnover, Life Care — ever since it was conceived in the heart and mind of Forrest Preston — has always been about the Dorothy Giehms of this land.

Often, as he and I travel to a nursing center (and he visits them often, and encourages corporate leadership to do likewise), a planned stay of 45 minutes turns into four hours. The first order of business always is to visit the residents — to hug them, to squeeze their hands, to ask how they are, and to determine if they are being treated well.

People don't go to a nursing center to die; they go there to live. Life Care was created to meet the needs of those in our care, but, even more, to enrich the quality of the time they spend with us. Hence, the name of this book. It is a celebration of life — and of those who have tasted it and relished it.

Yes, Forrest Preston has a passion for his life's calling. This book is about his dream, and his continuing pursuit of it. But more than that, it honors the wonderful men and women, each with an interesting story, who populate Life Care's centers all across the country. It is also a tribute to the exceptional associates who, too, see their work as a ministry in the lives of God's children.

We acknowledge, with special appreciation, the talents of Barry Parker, honored with the Touchstone Award for writing, and Robin Hood, Pulitzer Prize-winning photographer. Their work on "The Tennesseans," two books about the people of our state, inspired the idea for this book. Their sojourn in our centers, and the people they encountered, in pursuit of the text and the images have profoundly affected their lives.

Beecher Hunter

Beecher Hunter

Executive Vice President

Corporate and Community Relations

The Story of Life Care

It all began with a long-shot, cold call. At 8 a.m. on a summer day in 1967, Forrest Preston and a friend, Farrell Jones, knocked at the door of a nursing home company in Wenatchee, Washington. They hadn't phoned the owner of the company, Carl Campbell, to say they were coming but had risked the drive to central Washington from Oregon the night before in hopes of seeing the businessman and presenting to him their venture idea. "We had blind faith we'd find him in," Preston recalls.

The door was locked, but moments later the lanky, soft-spoken Campbell rounded a corner of the office to arrive for work. He knew one of the men at his doorstep: Jones, an Oregon-based contractor, had done plastering and other exterior work for several of Campbell's nursing home projects. Campbell had never laid eyes on the 34-year-old Preston, who made his home 3,000 miles away in Cleveland, Tennessee.

Campbell had been raised in the Depression and had turned an industrious nature and knack for business into early success. After running a roofing company, he and an older brother, Willis, had built the first free-standing nursing home in Washington. In 1954, Campbell and his wife, Betty, opened the first of their own nursing homes. She was the registered nurse and cook; he was the bookkeeper and orderly, dishwasher and janitor. Their children helped as well. By 1967, the Campbells' hard work had blossomed into 25 nursing homes across the Northwest.

"Farrell, I feel badly, but I've got a full day planned," said Campbell, when told his early morning visitors wanted to discuss a nursing home proposal with him. He explained he would be piloting a single-

Depicting a true Life Care story, the nurse presenting a rose to a nursing home resident became the company symbol.

engine plane on an inspection tour of several of his nursing centers in Washington and Idaho communities. Then the congenial Campbell paused, thought a moment, and said: "However, if you guys aren't afraid to fly with me, we can talk about your project as we go, and we'll be on our way."

Preston and Jones jumped at the chance. In the plane's small cabin during a morning of short flights, they described their vision. They wanted to build a nursing home in Cleveland that would elevate the quality of long-term care in that community and rival any nursing center in the nation. The facility would be attractively furnished and staffed by well-trained, highly motivated personnel. It would offer engaging activities, foster warm friendships and create an environment where residents were treated with dignity and respect, not warehoused to die.

But the two young businessmen lacked the resources to make the dream come true. They needed financial backing, and they hoped that Campbell, a successful nursing home entrepreneur, would embrace their idea and co-sign a bank note in return for part ownership of the facility in the southern community.

Campbell was intrigued. "Farrell, I know you do good work and that you're dependable," he said. "I don't know Forrest, though I do know of his family." The elder Prestons lived in neighboring Oregon, and Campbell had heard Forrest's father, the Reverend Benjamin Preston, a Seventh-day Adventist minister, speak on several occasions. There was something, too, about Forrest Preston that attracted Campbell. "He had a lot of fire," says Campbell, remembering that day, "and he was quite a talker, even then. I liked him immediately."

Though a generation apart in age, Campbell and Preston shared deep values and formative experiences. The families of both men had offered them a strong religious upbringing. Both had older brothers whom they joined in business at the start of their careers. Both men combined entrepreneurial gifts and compassionate natures. And, both had seen conditions in centers for the elderly that would shape the course of their lives. Campbell's experience occurred as a teenager when he and his brothers sang in a church band for residents of a county poor farm in his native Washington. "You're impressionable at that age," he says. "The smells, the conditions they lived in, made an indelible impression."

That afternoon the trio landed at Coeur d'Alene, Idaho, across the Washington border, where Campbell was building a nursing home, and continued their discussion over sandwiches at a drive-in restaurant north of town. Seated at an outdoor table under a canopy, Campbell made his decision. "I think you guys would be honest and fair with me," he said, "and I think you can make this happen." In a leap of faith in his young companions, he agreed to support their venture in far-away Cleveland.

Campbell soon visited Cleveland where he was greeted by a gracious and grateful Preston. On the strength of Campbell's commitment to the venture, the trio was able to borrow $305,000 from the Cleveland National Bank to move the project forward. "For us, it was like striking a gold mine because he (Campbell) was willing to trust us," Preston would later declare of the man

who became a personal friend as well as partner and mentor. "In his own God-given, talented way, Carl has based his entire life on trusting other people."

At the bottom of page one of the Friday, January 2, 1970 edition of the *Cleveland (Tenn.) Daily Banner* is a photo of Forrest Preston beside a story announcing the grand opening of Garden Terrace Convalescent Center. The article describes the 99-bed nursing home — perched on a wooded, seven-acre tract overlooking Keith Street on the outskirts of Cleveland — as a "showplace facility with carpets and chandeliers." The dedication was set for 2 p.m. that Sunday.

The article declares that the skilled nursing care center, the fruit of the Preston-Campbell-Jones venture, will offer professional medical care, rehabilitation equipment, recreational programs, meals planned by a dietitian, beauty and barber services, and a television in every resident's room. Forrest Preston is identified as the administrator.

This wasn't exactly the profession Benjamin and Ethel Preston envisioned for their youngest son, though not too far afield, either. They hoped Forrest would become a physician and expected his older brother, Winton, to be the entrepreneur in the family. Winton obliged, attending Seventh-day Adventist-run Southern Missionary College (now Southern University) near Cleveland while his parents lived in Atlanta. He then pursued a childhood fascination with printing presses by opening Preston Printing, a high-quality custom printing company, in Cleveland.

Meanwhile, the rest of the Preston family, including two daughters, moved to Oregon, sending 14-year-old Forrest to boarding school at Upper Columbia Academy in Spangle, Washington, 30 miles from Spokane. More interested in roaming than studying, the inquisitive, energetic Preston

GROUND BREAKING
MONDAY, APRIL 7, 1969
GRAND OPENING
SUNDAY, JAN. 4, 1970
Contractor
DEVELOPMENT ENTERPRISES, INC.
Architect
DON R. KIRKMAN

held a variety of school jobs — nightwatchman, volunteer fireman, dairy plant workman, among others — that gave him access to every corner of the campus.

He declared a premedical major at Walla Walla College in Washington but soon abandoned the idea of becoming a physician, feeling that the practice of medicine was too confining a focus for his wide-ranging interests. At the same time, to help pay tuition, he became a part-time, door-to-door salesman for the Electrolux vacuum cleaner company. Before long, he was earning a reputation for outselling full-time employees. By once selling a cleaner to a woman whose home had no electricity, he entered company lore, though this wasn't the heartless act it seemed, for her house was about to be wired. His ability to easily engage strangers in conversation and win them over and his penchant for delivering more than they expected were attributes that pointed to his future success.

Nonetheless, Preston continued to pursue a health career, earning certification as an x ray technologist from the California College of Medical Technology in San Gabriel. Over the next three years, he worked for two hospitals and a physician's office.

But in 1957, at the age of 24, he changed direction, accepting Winton's invitation to join him in the Cleveland printing company he had built. As he traveled to Tennessee, Forrest carried a valuable idea with him. Noticing that hospitals of the day provided poorly produced information booklets for patients and their families, he saw a potentially large, new market for Winton's presses to fill. The brothers subsequently co-founded Hospital Publications, Incorporated, to design and print custom hospital booklets. Winton oversaw production and Forrest served as vice president of sales and development.

Brimming with a natural salesman's exuberance and confidence, Forrest Preston crisscrossed the country, calling on hospitals coast to coast and sending back sales orders to Cleveland. In the next 12 years, Hospital

Ethel Preston with sons, Forrest, right, and Winton. The brothers worked together before Forrest founded Life Care.

Publications became a leader in its field, supplying a sizable percentage of the nation's hospitals with printed materials. By the time he left Winton in 1969 to devote himself full-time to the nursing home business, Forrest Preston headed a highly successful, 17-person national sales force that he had built.

During sales calls on hospitals, he sometimes visited their affiliated nursing homes and began to consider them a market for patient booklets as well. More importantly, though, he witnessed in some a shocking level of care. They were unattractive and poorly maintained, often filled with flies and the stench of soiled clothing. Listless residents suffered from a lack of stimulating activity and warm, human contact. Preston felt long-term care should be delivered in far more humane, pleasant and productive surroundings by a trained, compassionate staff.

He shared his idea with Farrell Jones, who had been a classmate two years ahead of Preston at Upper Columbia Academy and Walla Walla College and who was now in the construction business. The two began talking of building and managing a small, trend-setting nursing home in Cleveland. While on a cross-country vacation trip with his young family, Preston visited Jones at his Oregon home and agreed to try meeting Carl Campbell on that fateful summer day in 1967 in an effort to enlist his support in the project.

With Carl Campbell's backing, construction had begun on Garden Terrace in Cleveland. From directing the pouring of footings to the selection of drapes, Preston was a dervish of activity. Periodically, he'd stop at the office of the *Cleveland Daily Banner* to share his excitement with Associate Editor Beecher Hunter. "His enthusiasm for the project was contagious," Hunter recalls. "Whenever I visited the construction trailer, he would roll

Entrepreneur Carl Campbell enabled Forrest Preston to establish Life Care and became his mentor and friend.

and make it the best it possibly could be, and then go and repeat that success. When that is done, growth will take care of itself."

And it did. Development Enterprises, Inc., the company Preston, Campbell and Jones created to develop Garden Terrace and other nursing home and real estate projects, was soon busy constructing a nursing home in Tullahoma, Tennessee, 90 miles from Cleveland. Named Meadows Convalescent Center, it opened in September 1970.

In October 1970, the trio opened The Village Greene in Greeneville, Tennessee, followed in June 1973 by Hallmark Center in Morristown, Tennessee. All three facilities were within a two-hour drive of Cleveland. The fledgling company extended its geographic reach by opening Heritage Center in Altamonte Springs, Florida, in December 1974. Returning to Tennessee, Development Enterprises dedicated The Village Center in the nearby Chattanooga suburb of East Ridge in June 1975. The names of each of the original six, and many subsequent centers, later carried the prefix, Life Care Center, followed by the name of the community it was in.

A center-by-center immersion in the nursing home business enabled Life Care to give personal attention to the construction, staffing and operation of each facility. There was the opportunity to evaluate and refine policies, activities and amenities. Core values had time to take root. The most important of these values — resident satisfaction — was illustrated in Preston's dictum to the staff to "always keep the boss happy." And the boss, he was quick to add, was not Preston but "each and every resident in our nursing centers."

By 1976, Development Enterprises had opened the six nursing homes, totaling 881 beds, in two states, and the need arose for a long-term care management company to operate them.

To accomplish this, Life Care Centers of America, Incorporated, was co-founded by Preston, Campbell and Jones in

out blueprints and walk me through the site." Hunter, who would later become Life Care's executive vice president, attended the grand opening in January 1970. "When I saw the final product, even after all the preparation I had witnessed, I was amazed," he says. "This was the Hyatt Regency of Cleveland business developments."

The nursing home gained immediate acceptance. Family members were impressed by its attractive contrast to the stark decor of nursing homes of the day and by the caring attitude of its staff. Residents quickly filled the 99 beds. As administrator, Preston was able to assure the quality of its operations and gain invaluable, hands-on experience. From the beginning, he would later say, the plan was to "build a single facility

Life Care Across America
1976

Cleveland on January 6, 1976. The company's name signaled its philosophy of caring for elders of a community so they might enjoy the fullness of their lives, not mark time until their passing. The name also announced Life Care's intention to build a national health system. The company declared as its mission: "Providing the highest quality of service to those who entrust their lives or the lives of their loved ones to our care."

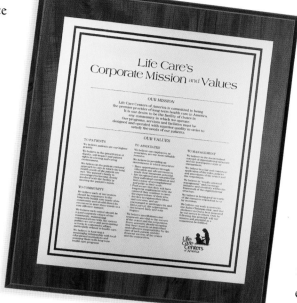

From the start, the mission and values statement were prominently posted in centers for residents, family members and associates to see.

From the beginning, Life Care embraced a set of management principles that ran counter to the approach of most American businesses. The "bottom line" at Life Care was not defined as growth and profits, as necessary as they were to the corporation's success. Rather the focus was on meeting the needs — physical, emotional, social and spiritual — of every resident. If that was achieved, went Life Care's thinking, corporate success would follow. "We have never set goals based on the quantity of beds or volume of dollars," Preston declared some years later. "The goals were always predicated upon the excellence of the health care we provide."

From its earliest days, Life Care attracted to its ranks people with an altruistic approach to business. "This company is about good patient care; it's the first thing they talk about when you go to a meeting," says J. Anderson Greene, executive director at Life Care Center of Banner Elk in North Carolina. "The goal is always about putting the resident first. This is what sets Life Care apart from other nursing home companies."

Life Care's relationship with staff members was enlightened and unusual for corporate America. Instead of top-down management that relied on authority and intimidation to achieve results, Life Care adopted an inverted pyramid management style that placed the corporate-office team at the bottom, not dictating to but working in support of those who delivered day-to-day, hands-on care.

"Those in the field are the most important; they're where the action is," explains Life Care Executive Vice President Beecher Hunter. "Next come the regional and divisional staffs and, finally, the corporate staff, who function as servant leaders." He adds: "The really great people in this company are the executive directors, the department heads and all the associates, particularly the directors of nursing, the CNAs (certified nursing assistants) and volunteers of the centers who interact with residents every day. They deliver the care with love and compassion."

Toward these people Life Care developed a culture of encouragement and appreciation. All employees came to be called "associates," an egalitarian term indicating that everyone in the company, from a chef at a center to the chairman and owner, belonged to the same close-knit, mutually respecting team working toward a single, lofty goal. Over the years, an array of coveted awards was established to

Teamwork quickly became a Life Care trademark, whether in the nursing homes or a corporate softball league.

recognize associates who contributed at an exceptional level in their various roles.

In 1976, the newly created Life Care organization held its first annual management meeting in a small room at a Cleveland Holiday Inn, with 25 attending. So began a company tradition that would grow to include hundreds of executive directors and spouses flown in from around the

country at company expense each fall for a gala, five-day program of inspirational addresses by nationally known speakers, corporate reports on goals and results, team-building activities, and high-spirited entertainment.

"The annual meeting is not just a sharing of technical information," Beecher Hunter explains. "Like an old-time church camp meeting, it emphasizes motivation and fellowship. In being together, we realize we all face problems and challenges, but we're family and can share our help and support. That's of inestimable value."

The camp-meeting analogy captures the spirit of Life Care's annual gathering. In the secular corporate world, Life Care was and is an anomaly: a non-religious organization that openly espouses Biblical values and ethics. The Golden Rule is cited as the perspective to bring to care (treat the resident as you would want yourself or a loved one treated), and the work of associates is described as a ministry. Associates of many faiths enjoy the sense of a higher calling that Life Care instills in their work.

——❦——

Life Care Centers of America was in its infancy in the late 1970s when Angelena Clayton drove by the company's 5,000-square-foot corporate office on Keith Street each morning on her way to work. "It was such a pretty building, and it looked so serene when I passed it," she recalls. "I used to wonder what was going on." When she came to work for Life Care as administrative assistant to Forrest Preston in August 1980, she found a beehive of activity behind the placid facade. "I didn't walk into a dull, routine job," she says. "You never knew what the day would bring."

The only predictable aspect of Life Care's corporate life was growth. After building the original six centers in Tennessee and Florida and incorporating as Life Care in 1976, the company had constructed or acquired centers in locations as distant as Paducah, Kentucky, and Hilo,

Hawaii. The number of Life Care-managed beds jumped each year: from 1,047 in 1977, to 1,655 in 1978, to 2,626 in 1979. When Angie Clayton arrived in 1980, Life Care could claim 24 managed facilities across America with 3,184 beds and net revenues of $30 million.

As it grew, Life Care followed its "do it right each time" philosophy. At the same time, the company searched for dramatic opportunities to bring its formula for nursing home success to other markets in the country.

This required nimble action and nerves of steel. Because the critical factors, including interest rates, construction costs and health care regulations, that affect the climate for building or buying centers were constantly changing, planning had to be done on a monthly, daily, even minute-to-minute basis. And because Life Care was small, much was riding on each decision.

Life Care facilities opened constantly as the young company entered new markets to fill the growing need for high-quality, long-term care.

Retirement centers joined nursing homes on Life Care campuses as the company broadened its mission to provide specialized accommodations for older residents not requiring nursing care.

Spotting new trends, finding opportunities for growth, and inspiring each center to be the best in its community was the work of Forrest Preston, who now sat as sole owner of Life Care. Farrell Jones had sold his shares in Development Enterprises and Life Care in the late 1970s to form his own company, and Carl Campbell would sell his assets to Preston in 1982 to concentrate on further development of his nursing home system and other businesses.

One trend Life Care had already spotted was the growing need for retirement centers for those elderly who, unlike nursing home residents requiring round-the-clock nursing care, could live independently or with modest assistance in apartments. In 1979, Life Care created an affiliate, Retirement Centers of America, Inc., to manage retirement living facilities for the company. The first management contract was with Cheyenne Place Retirement Center in Colorado Springs.

Meanwhile, Life Care continued adding to its family of nursing homes. Some were built solely by Life

Care and others received backing from local investors. Still other centers were purchased from nursing home organizations that were divesting themselves of facilities. In 1981, acquisitions in Nebraska and Colorado increased Life Care's managed bed count to 3,622 in 27 centers. By 1982, the number had grown to 3,985 beds at 31 centers. That year Life Care created another sister company, Life Care Affiliates, to deal with the growing volume of acquisitions, a function previously handled by a small in-house department.

Each new center carried the Life Care imprint. Physically, they were attractively furnished and sparkling clean. The grounds were groomed and planted with native flowers and shrubs. Maintenance was a priority and attention to detail a requirement. This reflected Preston's own penchant for beauty and order. "I think I'm pretty observant," says Angie Clayton, Preston's long-time administrative assistant, "but he can walk into a room and see something out of place I never noticed."

As he toured the nursing homes of the growing company, Preston preached the gospel of compassionate care and the worth and dignity of the individual. In concrete ways, he demonstrated these beliefs. During a visit to one nursing home, he discovered, to his dismay, that belongings of recently deceased residents were routinely stuffed in bags for the family to claim. "Forrest felt the way we honor the dead says a lot about how we cared for them while they were alive," says Hunter, recounting the story. Upon returning to Cleveland, Preston had Life Care's marketing department produce a specially designed box so final belongings could be neatly folded and presented to the grieving family. A card of condolence accompanied the box.

When Preston and other members of the management team visited centers around the country, they met first with residents, sharing hugs and conversation, before attending to operational issues. "You are blessed when you visit a nursing home," Preston would say. "You receive more than you give." In later years, residents would be profiled in the company's magazine and invited to corporate functions. The respect the company owner showed residents and the pleasure he took in meeting them sent a clear message through the organization.

While Life Care's mission was defined by the quality care each resident received, corporate success could be measured in surging growth. In 1983, Life Care claimed 40 facilities with a combined 5,489 beds. By 1984, there were 59 facilities with 8,085 beds in 15 states. In 1985, the number climbed to 76 facilities and 9,629 beds; net revenue of $144 million was almost five times greater than in 1980.

In 1986, as the company celebrated its tenth anniversary, there were 90 Life Care owned or managed nursing centers and eight retirement centers in 21 states, from Massachusetts to Hawaii, and the 881 beds that existed ten years before had grown to nearly 10,000. "As we grew, Mr. Preston would continue to say: 'We're just a small company,'" recalls Angie Clayton. "And I'm thinking, 'We're not so small anymore.'"

———————

The tenth anniversary was an occasion to reaffirm Life Care's goals. "The challenge we have had over the past ten years is to assure our patients and their families

that our overriding commitment to quality remains our greatest concern," Preston declared. "We need to make this the most vivid fact for our families to see." He stressed the need for constant improvement. "We're always seeking to do better at each location — to learn from those things that are working well and apply them to those that are not." And he praised "a spirit among the people of Life Care that is readily noticeable. It's somewhat like a torch," he added. "You can stand still and hold it and burn yourself, or you can run with it and pass it on."

Racing with the torch was what Life Care associates were doing. The company had opened one facility, at Payson, in the competitive Arizona long-term health care market in 1985 and in 1986 opened five more: in Prescott, Sierra Vista, Yuma, Tucson and Scottsdale. The expansion campaign was an impressive example of Life Care's growing confidence and strength. "Everywhere we have gone, we've been the shining example of what the nursing home industry should be," declared a Life Care regional director, who accurately predicted that Arizona Life Care facilities would gain ascendancy in their markets.

Similarly, the name of Life Care's new, full-color, quarterly magazine, *Life Care Leader*, reflected the company's goal of striving not to be the biggest nursing center chain in America, but the best. "It *(Leader)* will spotlight the unique and wonderful men and women who live in our centers and who have delightful and moving stories to

The premier issue of Life Care Leader set the tone for a magazine which celebrated those who lived and worked in Life Care centers.

tell," said Preston in the June 1986 inaugural issue. "It will present the achievements of those in the Life Care family who have dedicated themselves to the enrichment of the lives of the elderly. *Life Care Leader* will be a celebration of life."

The creator and editor of the magazine, former newspaper editor Beecher Hunter, joined Life Care in 1986 after watching Forrest Preston's idea for a better nursing home flourish. Serving together in Cleveland's Jaycees organization and the community's YMCA building program, he and Preston developed a personal friendship. "Forrest and I shared the same beliefs and values," said Hunter. "When I came to Life Care, I enjoyed his strong support and mentoring and felt he wanted me to help define and communicate Life Care's culture."

Besides the *Leader*, Hunter continued the company newsletter, *The Exchange;* started a column, *Life Times,* that could be placed by nursing centers in their local papers; created newsletters for Life Care's medical directors and other segments of the Life Care family; and used impressive multiple-projector slide programs and videotapes as teaching and motivation tools. One video, "Angels Among Us," was taped in ten locations, from nursing center lobbies to a snowy forest in Colorado, and included a choir of 135 children singing atop a mountain in Tennessee.

The challenge for Hunter and all the Life Care staff was to maintain a passionate focus on caring for the individual even as the company grew large and spread across America. The corporate communications program made this a priority. In one issue of *The Leader,* Hunter described a poignant moment — the admission of a loved one to a nursing home — as a way of putting a human face on Life Care's mission:

"She was a distinguished lady," he wrote in the editor's column, "with a classic face and splashes of gray in her hair. She was well dressed. Appearance, it was obvious, was important to her. But exhaustion was written all over her face. She walked uncertainly into the lobby of Life

Colorado Governor Roy Romer opens Life Care's Garden Terrace Alzheimer's Center of Excellence in the Denver suburb of Aurora, the first freestanding Alzheimer's center in that state.

Care Center of East Ridge, Tennessee, and sank down into a chair. She was tired, forlorn and confused.

"Joy Hambleton, the administrator, appeared in the lobby en route to her office. She noticed the woman sitting there, and her heart went out to her. Ms. Hambleton walked over and put her arm around her and said, 'I'm so sorry.' The visitor leaned her head on Ms. Hambleton's shoulder, her body crumpled like a little doll's, and she began crying. She had come to admit her husband, and the experience was very emotional.

"The couple had no children, and she had no sisters or brothers. 'He's all I've got and all I've ever had,' she told Ms. Hambleton. Now, with his health declining, she knew she could no longer care for her husband at home. A nursing home was her only alternative. 'Well, if you come here, we can all be your family,' Ms. Hambleton responded. 'I think,' Ms. Hambleton related later, 'that's the way a lot of families feel. Admitting a loved one to a nursing home is a deeply moving experience, and we need to be sensitive to that.'"

---

*T*he gathering of Life Care associates for the annual management meeting in Cleveland in 1987 was a homecoming. Only three of these meetings had been held in Cleveland since 1976 (sites had ranged from Florida to Colorado to Hawaii), but this year was different. Life Care

When completed in Cleveland, Tennessee in 1987, Life Care's Corporate Plaza consolidated the functions of the company headquarters on one campus and provided accommodations for the company's large national meetings.

had begun developing its Corporate Plaza, an interconnected complex of attractive wood-and-stone buildings that, for the first time, gave the company the auditorium capacity (seating 500) and banquet space (seating 450) to host the company's important and festive national gathering.

The new corporate campus, located adjacent to the former Life Care office building on Keith Street, was "a dream come true" for Preston. "As far back as 12 years ago," he said, "it was my hope to be able to develop a training facility where we could enjoy such events as the management meetings, along with workshops and seminars."

It also allowed Life Care to consolidate corporate offices, then spread among several Cleveland locations, in one highly functional setting. The spacious complex included the three-story

Operations Center, where corporate offices were housed; the Growth Center, a two-story building for Life Care Affiliates and other Life Care departments; the Professional Development Center, with its large meeting spaces; and the Welcome Center, where the Life Care story could be impressively communicated to visitors.

Working in the Corporate Plaza were men and women of talent and dedication. From its beginning, Life Care counted on a strong corporate-level team to help associates around the country build the best long-term health care company in America. Bud Stout and Desmond Cummings had served in top management posts in Life Care's formative years. Dr. Ben Wygal, Tom Winston and Ned Wilford continued the tradition of leadership, each increasing the company's ability to fulfill

Life Care Across America
1985

its mission of enriching the lives of those it served. Life Care was the recipient of the skilled efforts of many other individuals, some of whom later began nursing home companies of their own.

To keep pace with the growth of facilities across the country, the company created new divisions and regions to oversee operations. Each division and region had its own staff, charged with helping the individual centers achieve superiority in their markets. This corporate structure wasn't stifling, for individual centers maintained a large degree of autonomy in their business activities. At the same time that Life Care was spreading geographically, the company was seeking ways to extend its continuum of services through such programs as sub-acute care, geriatric day care, and care for persons with Alzheimer's disease.

Far from staying on the new corporate campus, Preston and his home office colleagues made it a point to travel as often as they could to centers around the country. Whether it was to present an award or just say, hello, Life

Care's officers were frequently on the road. "He (Preston) enjoys the people part of the work, of visiting the centers," notes Administrative Assistant Angie Clayton. "Nobody can inspire associates in the field like he can. There's something about the founder of the company taking time to visit a facility and talk to residents and staff that is very special."

Maintaining the personal touch was a Life Care priority. It could be seen in the practice of having the company's chairman and its president personally respond in writing to all complaints addressed to the corporate office and in making customer service everybody's business. It was evident in the field. "When Forrest comes to visit," says associate Jerry Weeter, "it's not with an entourage of accountants. He doesn't come to the office first; he goes straight to the residents to press the flesh. And if it's an event we're having, he's the last to leave. What a role model!"

Life Care, itself, was a model for corporate success. By 1988, it had become the ninth largest company in the nation providing long-term health care, operating

91 centers representing 12,451 beds. Two years later, in 1990, on the 20th anniversary of the original Garden Terrace Convalescent Center (renamed Life Care Center of Cleveland), the company managed 120 nursing centers in 26 states. As a salute to the first center, the Garden Terrace name became the prefix for Life Care's new Alzheimer's Centers of Excellence. The first opened in 1990 in the Denver suburb of Aurora with Colorado Governor Roy Romer delivering the keynote address.

As Life Care celebrated its 15th anniversary in 1991, the company could point to a sterling record of achievement. It now operated 131 nursing centers in 26 states, offering 17,855 long-term care beds. Its retirement center division, renamed American Lifestyles, managed 14 facilities representing 2,154 apartments. The company had scheduled its first national satisfaction survey to measure performance. And more than 450 associates and guests attending the annual management meeting in Cleveland that year shouted, "Good Morning, America," in an ABC television-style format.

The nation was awake to Life Care's presence.

---

*I*n his column in the company newsletter, *The Exchange*, Forrest Preston often used real-life examples to illustrate such Life Care values as pride in one's work and respect for the dignity of the individual. One homily concerned Charles Schwab, a steel executive, who earned a million-dollar salary before World War II. Asked what made him so valuable, Schwab confessed it wasn't his knowledge of steel-making; many people knew more than he. It was, he said, his ability to arouse enthusiasm in employees. Schwab declared: "The way to develop the best in a person is by appreciation and encouragement."

It was a belief Preston had always placed at the heart of Life Care's management program, but in 1992 the company formalized its efforts to honor associates who displayed exceptional dedication to their work. The "Whatever It Takes" customer service campaign was introduced to recognize those who went the extra mile to help residents and their families. Each center named a winner, based on a specific act of service; that winner then competed for the divisional honor and a $1,000 prize. Throughout the company, associates wore red-white-and-blue "Whatever It Takes" buttons proclaiming their willingness to serve.

Life Care also began its presentation of performance awards at the annual management meeting. The Chairman's Award, President's Award, Corporate Award, Personal Service Award and Facility of the Year Award were bestowed to the applause of fellow associates. The Carl W. Campbell Wind Beneath My Wings Award, honoring Life Care's volunteer of the year, was soon added to the company honors. Award winners are routinely treated to a six-day retreat and personal growth event at a Florida resort, Useppa Island.

Life Care's goal is for every associate to feel like a winner. For executive directors, that experience occurs in a visible way as soon as they land in Chattanooga for the

Recognition is paramount at Life Care where an array of annual awards was established to honor associates and volunteers for exceptional service.

CARL W. CAMPBELL
YOU ARE THE WIND BENEATH MY WINGS
FORREST L. PRESTON
PRESENTED SEPTEMBER 23, 1992

short drive to Cleveland for their annual fall meeting. At the airport gate are Forrest Preston and other members of the management team to greet them. "He (Preston) hugs everyone who comes off the plane," says associate Lauren Gandara. "He knows everyone by name. He carries your bags. During the conference he came up to me and said: 'I'm so proud of you, kiddo.' That made me feel on top of the world."

The appreciation is genuine, for Life Care's corporate staff understands the emotional and physical rigors of nursing home work and the dedication required to do it well. A financial consultant struck a raw nerve when he proposed that Life Care electronically deposit payroll checks in associates' bank accounts as a time-saving, cost-cutting measure. Preston spoke in opposition, declaring he never wanted to create a situation where a supervisor did not personally hand a check to an associate and directly express appreciation for the work performed.

Keeping business personal remained Life Care's passion, even

as the company enjoyed exponential growth. By 1994, Life Care was managing 157 nursing and retirement centers in 27 states. There were five divisions and 20,000 associates. Yet, Beth Cliett didn't feel lost. She was then a newly hired associate participating in Life Care's five-day orientation program for executive directors held in Cleveland. Preston and other Life Care executives make it a priority to join these programs in session, and he was having breakfast with Cliett and her colleagues one morning.

Upon leaving her previous employer, a smaller nursing home company, she had been warned that she'd be lost in a "giant national chain" like Life Care. "It's interesting," she said with a smile to those around the table, "that I'm sitting next to the chairman of the company, and he does know who I am."

Understanding the changing health needs of America's soaring elderly population was critical to Life Care's success. One need was rehabilitation for those too disabled by injury to return home but not requiring an acute-care hospital room. To this end, Life Care created its subacute centers of excellence within nursing homes, the first opening at Life Care Center of Aurora in Colorado in 1994. Equipped with a gym and staffed by certified physical and occupational therapists, these specialized wings within nursing facilities enabled people to mend during short-term stays.

Life Care further extended its continuum of care by acquiring its first home health care agencies in 1996. By 1998, the company had formed Life Care at Home and was operating the affiliate in eight states. Upon a physi-

For Life Care associates who excelled at their posts, a company cruise was the reward.

health care as a career path. It did so through scholarships to college and university students and grants to foundations affiliated with state health care associations.

One of its first acts was to award scholarships through the Foundation's Benjamin M. and Ethel Preston Memorial Fund, named for Forrest Preston's parents. Life Care Associates and friends themselves pledged nearly $40, 000 to the special fund. Through April 2000, the Foundation made grants totaling more than $2 million to support 642 scholarship awards on 141 campuses in 35 states. Awards went to majors in health care administration and business administration, nursing, occupational therapy and physical therapy.

One of the most touching gifts from Life Care came in the form of a simple shoe box filled with toys and other

During Life Care's 20th anniversary celebration, Forrest Preston presented a logo statue to Tennessee Congresswoman Marilyn Lloyd.

cian's referral, Life Care at Home's staff evaluated a patient's needs and provided services, from rehabilitation therapy, wound care and other skilled nursing care to assistance with Medicare claims and private insurance forms. Life Care also continued to add retirement and assisted living facilities under American Lifestyles' banner, offering 32 of these attractive accommodations by 1998.

Life Care was not only developing new lines of business. As the company celebrated its 20th anniversary in 1996 with 180 nursing homes and 22,000 associates in 28 states, it was finding ways to share its success by giving to others. Two years earlier, the Life Care Foundation for Education and Research had been established to promote long-term

items for a child. It all began when Forrest Preston and his wife, Kathleen, saw a television program about Operation Christmas Child, an effort by Franklin Graham, son of the Rev. Billy Graham, to send gifts to children in war-torn countries at the holiday season. Moved by the purpose of the gifts and the pleasure they bestowed, the Prestons addressed Life Care's management meeting in 1995, asking if executive directors would have their centers participate in the annu-

Life Care Across America
1992

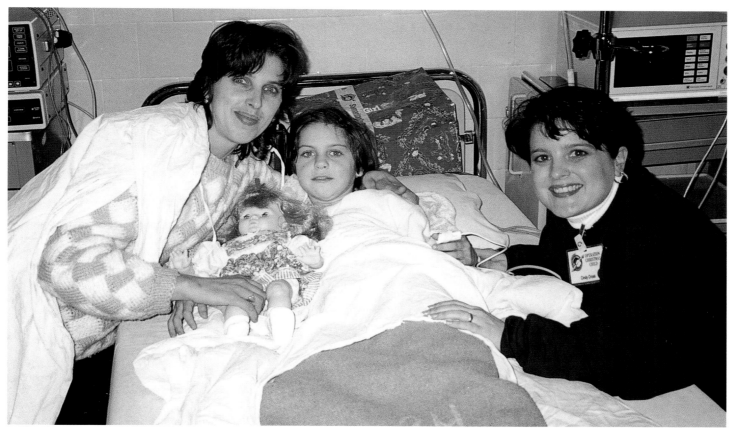

Life Care associate Cindy Cross (right) personally delivers Operation Christmas Child presents to a terminally ill patient in a children's hospital in Bucharest as her mother looks on.

al event. The answer was an enthusiastic, "Yes."

Beginning with 19,483 shoe boxes collected by associates for children in Bosnia, Rawanda and Croatia in 1995, the annual total climbed to 96,288 shoe boxes by 1999. Associates filled and wrapped boxes themselves and also enlisted the help of schools and civic groups in their communities. The boxes were placed beneath the Christmas trees in Life Care centers before they were collected by truck, then shipped overseas.

In an annual drawing, several associates were selected to accompany the gifts to their final destinations, a deeply moving experience they shared with their Life Care colleagues in the pages of the *Leader* and *The Exchange*. Accepting on behalf of the Life Care family, Preston received the Distinguished

Franklin Graham, left, director of Operation Christmas Child, with Life Care Executive Vice President Beecher Hunter and his wife, Lola.

Professional Service Award from the Tennessee Health Care Association for the success of the company's Operation Christmas Child campaign.

Life Care began its second 20 years in 1997 with the acquisition of three facilities on January 1, bringing the company to more than 200 nursing and retirement centers in 28 states. New divisions continued to be added; the list now included: New England, Central, Great Lakes, Eastern, Southwest, Mountain States and Pacific. Life Care Centers of America stretched from sea to shining sea.

Working with Preston was John O'Brien, who served as company president from 1995 to 1999. O'Brien previously served as Life Care's executive vice president and had risen through the ranks after joining the company fresh from college in 1984. His personal association with Forrest Preston began in 1977 when O'Brien was a 16-year-old high school junior working the summer in a Cleveland car wash that Preston owned as a side venture of Development Enterprises.

"It was a state-of-the-art facility," recalls O'Brien. "There probably hadn't been one that modern in the Southeast. We had a great group of people, and we were proud to work there. The attention to detail, the emphasis on quality: these traits are pervasive in all he (Preston) does." Preston was just as impressed with the young O'Brien's attitude and work ethic and offered him a job at Life Care upon graduation from college with business and CPA degrees.

While president, O'Brien visited about 75 facilities and divisional and regional offices a year. "For the management team to travel often, meeting associates and residents, being on the floor, is the best way to assure we stay in touch with our core business," he explained. "It's valuable for us to communicate the mission and challenges to associates in a very personal way. The opportunity to meet and work with so many good people is one I welcome."

Preston fostered a sense of family and esprit de corps among Life Care's more than 23,000 associates. One important bond was the array of separate annual meetings for executive directors, directors of nursing, medical directors, investors, and bankers. Divisional and regional meetings provided another opportunity for neighboring

nursing home staffs to share experiences, advice and support. Life Care's powerful videotapes were premiered at meetings and distributed throughout the corporation, instilling a sense of mission. So did the richly produced and widely circulated *Life Care Leader*, whose colorful pages inspired associates with stories of service.

Laughter was a powerful bond for Life Care associates. Offbeat moments at annual meetings became cherished tales. Take the time two harpists, both engaged, by mistake, to perform at the same event, almost came to blows over who would stay (both did). Or the time a ceiling sprinkler accidentally doused the massive, group photo shot at the end of a meeting. Then there was the time Preston tried to halt a spirited staff game of touch football that he was refereeing upon suddenly realizing what an injury might cost the company's self-insured health care program. The staff, including some beefy members, adamantly played on.

Preston, himself, provides a self-effacing brand of humor that endears him to associates. He has dressed in lederhosen for a meeting with a Bavarian theme and worn loud Hawaiian prints at company luaus. At one meeting, as a group gathered at poolside, the temptation became too great for several associates who tossed in their fully dressed chairman, to gales of laughter.

Best remembered is his participation at an annual-meeting talent show. For years, Preston had worn a toupee, resisting playful urging from friends to remove it. Following several very good acts by talented associates, he took the stage with a saxophone and pantomimed playing a piece of

Forrest Preston and his wife, Kathleen, join the gaiety of an annual meeting by dressing for a party with a Bavarian theme.

music. He was rigged so that in the middle of the performance, his pants fell to his ankles, revealing red and white shorts, and a fish line attached to the toupee lifted it in time to the music, then yanked it off, as Preston hotly pursued it across the stage. It was a show stopper and a demonstration that at Life Care no one stood on a pedestal. This was family.

As the decade and century drew to a close, Life Care created a second corporate campus in Cleveland. In 1995, the company purchased a vacant, 280,000-square-foot shopping center that had opened 20 years earlier as Cleveland's second mall. Located on Keith Street half a mile from the Corporate Plaza, the mammoth building afforded space for Life Care's growing support services and two affiliated com-

panies: American Lifestyles and Media Resource Group. Over the next three years, the building was gutted by workmen who created custom space for each department. Vast indoor plantings brought beauty to the interior and a new exterior face and landscaped entrance transformed a once-derelict structure into impressive company headquarters.

What immediately attracts visitors inside the center is the giant, illuminated stained-glass display facing the main entrance. Titled "Faces of Aging," it depicts the stages of life, from childhood to old age, as represented by the actual faces of four generations of women in one family. The picture was conceived by a Denver photographer in 1983, and so impressed Forrest Preston

Workers assemble the large, stained-glass "Faces of Aging" panel after separate tiles were shipped from Oregon. Attending the mosaic's dedication in October 1997 were, from left, Dr. Duane Fletcher, the creator; his wife, Edith; Valerie Egzibher, a relative of the family featured in the image; and Forrest Preston.

Dominating the interior of Life Care's Campbell Center, the 22-foot-wide "Faces of Aging" display depicts Life Care's philosophy. A Japanese proverb accompanying it declares: "The sun setting is no less beautiful than the sun rising."

Life Care's original headquarters building was moved to the Campbell Center in 1999 to become a museum to aging, while construction of a retirement center was planned for the site it left behind.

with its powerful symbolism that he had Life Care obtain permanent rights to the picture. It is accompanied by the Japanese proverb: "The sun setting is no less beautiful than the sun rising."

In an act of faith, Preston commissioned a retired physician, Dr. Duane Fletcher of Roseburg, Oregon, to transform the photograph into the giant, 15-by-22-foot stained-glass display. A newcomer to stained-glass creations, Fletcher had produced only a few small works. But Preston was convinced he could accomplish the project. From his home workshop, Fletcher created the beautiful display, tile by tile, and the result was striking. The project seemed ordained, for not one of the painted glass tiles cracked in their long cross-country trip. Declared Preston at the unveiling: "This image will not allow anyone to pass without thinking about the aged in society and how this element of our population should be regarded."

The 1998 dedication of the second corporate campus as The Campbell Center gave Preston the opportunity to honor his benefactor, Carl Campbell, and his wife, Betty, and was a testament to their abiding, 30-year friendship. A year before, the Prestons and Campbells had jointly funded a project at Upper Columbia Academy in Spangle, Washington, where Preston attended high school. The result of that gift, The Campbell Administration Building, was named in honor of Carl and Betty Campbell.

"Forrest has a tremendous amount of energy, drive and ideas," says Campbell. "For example, he can look at an old shopping center and have a vision of what to do with it." He continues: "Forrest has a strong spirit and religious principles, and the good Lord seems to bless him. His successes go on and on. And I have been blessed by association with him."

Life Care Across America

2000

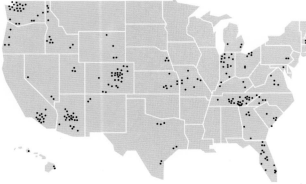

Cleveland residents could hardly believe their eyes when they saw the original Life Care headquarters building, which opened in 1976, inching down Keith Street. It was January 20, 1999, and the 20-ton building, straddling two tractor trailer beds, was bound for the southeast corner of The Campbell Center, where it would house an archives and museum. At the site it had occupied for 23 years would arise a five-story Life Care retirement center and assisted living facility.

It was an auspicious start to the last year of the decade and the century for Life Care. The company now claimed 230 nursing homes, retirement centers and assisted living centers in 28 states. There were 26,500 associates in what was the country's largest, privately owned nursing home company. And it had all started in the 5,000-square-foot building rolling inch by inch down Keith Street. Explaining Life Care's unusual lengths to save the building, Preston called it "the cradle" for much of America's long-term care industry. "For us, it has a lot of sentiment attached to it," he added.

Life Care's past and future were on display. The old headquarters would pay homage to a quarter-century of growth and progress. At its previous site, the new, $12 million independent and assisted living complex, called Garden Plaza Retirement Community in honor of Life Care's first center, which was still perched on the hill above it, would point to the future. With 174,000 square feet of space and a host of services and amenities, from a rehabilitation suite to a library, pool, spa and billiards room, it would create a campus of life-style choices for senior adults in southeast Tennessee.

In 1999, Michael Waddell was named president and chief executive officer of Life Care. The excitement of the position, he said, came from the opportunity to be "involved in a vision, the decision-making and implementation of plans that impact the lives of thousands of people in positive and meaningful ways."

Life Care was, indeed, affecting lives in positive and meaningful ways: In activity rooms of its nursing homes where people in their 90s discovered they were artists, in exercise rooms where they moved to music and laughter, during visits from family when they watched with an inner glow the generations that would be their legacy, in quiet moments when they savored life's warm memories and accomplishments.

Life Care was confronting and shaping the attitude Americans take toward their elders. In a culture that glorifies the young, the organization was asking people to look at the beauty that comes of experience and wisdom and a lifetime of challenges met. Associates were caregivers to the everyday heroes who fought the Great Wars and persevered in the Great Depression and built a country that was free and families that were strong.

Those who enter a Life Care center find that each resident has a story to tell and a lesson to share. "You are blessed when you visit," as Forrest Preston says. "You receive more than you give."

The Life Care Mission:

"Life Care Centers of America is committed to being the premier provider of long-term health care in America. It is our desire to be the facility of choice in any community in which we operate. Our programs, services and facilities must be designed and operated with superior quality in order to satisfy the needs of our residents.

A Day in the Life of Life Care

As morning sun first touches America, lighting the spars of trawlers in Massachusetts harbors and coloring sugary beaches on the Florida coast, life within the easternmost of Life Care's 250 centers is stirring.

At Life Care Center of Nashoba Valley, set on 43 acres of former orchard land a few miles northwest of Boston, Charlie makes his rounds. The resident golden retriever eagerly seeks the first hand of the day held palm up toward him and drops his muzzle in its support. Down the hallway, music is playing, and participants in the center's Fit For Your Life exercise program are stretching out the stiffness in their legs. "Up, point, flex, down; Up, point, flex, down," says their cheer-leading instructor. "Good extension. Excellent, kids."

The Nashoba Valley "kids" are proving that even in advanced age, the "use it or lose it" adage applies. They press light dumbbells overhead to tone upper body muscles and perform seated leg lifts to strengthen the torso. Following a university-designed exercise program for the elderly, they not only improve their strength and balance but their mood. Smiles and quips are an instant payoff.

"Here, Kitty Kitty! Here, Kitty Kitty!" Morning light slants through a window at Life Care Center at Hilliard north of Jacksonville, Florida, as BeeBee, the wise-cracking cockatiel perched on a cage at a nursing station, taunts the felines who live with him at the facility. The center has created an Eden environment of animals and plants that gives residents the responsibility of caring for life and the satisfaction this meaningful activity brings.

BeeBee and the cats are joined at the center by rabbits Flopsie and Mopsie; three other cockatiels, Lucy, Ricky and Gracie; greyhounds Buck and Dessie; Patch, a sheltie, and Joey, a terrier. Two geese, Frick and Frack, patrol a small pond outside the center where two dozen ducks and mallards splash-land throughout the day. The grandchildren of residents and school groups from the Hilliard community love to visit the center's menagerie, adding vitality to the residents' day.

Life Care is about living as fully and joyfully as possible. Innovative projects and activities at centers across America prove the point. "Many people feel broken — physically powerless and helpless when they first come to us," observes Angela Bialkowski, activity and marketing director at Life Care Center of Tucson, Arizona. "What is wonderful is to see how they regenerate and renew themselves here. There is a metamorphosis as they become active." She adds: "As long as a person is alive, life is self-actualizing. Age shouldn't be important."

Her center, surrounded by the stark desert beauty of rocks, cactus and craggy mountains, overflows with creative energy. Its walls are hung with art produced by residents: watercolors, acrylics and crochet

"Many people feel broken — physically powerless and helpless when they first come to us. What is wonderful is to see how they regenerate and renew themselves here."

Angela Bialkowski
Activity and Marketing Director, Life Care Center of Tucson, AZ

work; stuffed clowns and dolls made of papier-mache; colorful weavings and quilts. A woman on an outside deck tends violas in the brilliant morning light. Her face, contorted by arthritic pain, grows soft as she nurtures the delicate blossoms.

Getting residents into nature is a focus at many centers. At Life Care Center of Banner Elk in the Blue Ridge mountains of western North Carolina, residents take rides in a golf cart they helped purchase by making items, from birdhouses to quilts, that they sold at their Christmas bazaar. Down a gravel path from the center they travel in the cart into a setting of rolling hills and distant, hazy blue mountains.

"In the summer, we have a lemonade stand outside the front entrance and people take turns riding in the cart," says Director of Activities Kim Cuthbertson. "We picnic in the orchard, eating apples and collecting material for potpourri. One resident, she's German, said that with the wind and sun on her face, she hadn't felt this alive in years."

Music, too, enlivens the centers. Volunteer performers entertain in an array of styles. "Klondike Nell," flashy in a sequined jumpsuit and large-frame, purple glasses, belts out Ethel Merman stage-show tunes as residents celebrate a birthday at Hallmark Manor near Seattle, Washington. Bob Walker, a traveling "Music Man," plays such golden oldies as "My Blue Heaven" on the electronic keyboard at Life Care Center at Wells Crossing south of Jacksonville, Florida. As he sings, an assistant activity director at the center moves from one resident to another in their wheelchairs and holds their hands while dancing in perfect time to the music.

Residents make their own music. The Glee Club at Life Care Center at Paradise Valley in Scottsdale, Arizona, joins members of the Echo Mountain Elementary School Headstart program in an intergenerational rendition of "You Are My Sunshine." At Life Care Center of Corona east of Los Angeles, Joseph Wright, a former big-band musician, entertains fellow residents on the upright piano two nights a week. North of Seattle, at Life Care Center of Marysville, resident Agnes Benaugh uncorks operatic trills just as she did as a stage performer for many years.

If there's a way to engage residents in the excitement of the moment, Life Care has discovered it. Drawn in a circle and holding a large, colorful section of light parachute silk taut between them, residents of Life Care Center of Greeneville, Tennessee, play "Body Buster." The object is to keep a beach ball bouncing on the chute by waving your end of the silk sheet whenever the ball approaches. The game requires brisk shoulder and arm movement along with timing and concentration, all beneficial to muscles, nerves and joints. But it's the sport of it that makes the adrenalin flow. Shouts and cheers greet each volley.

Nostalgic remembrance can also rev the emotions. The Time Travel Club meets weekly at Life Care Center of Tucson. Trudy from California, Ann from Chicago, Lois from Ohio, Sophie from Michigan, Gill from New Jersey, Otto from Germany, Betty from Ireland and a half dozen more residents sit in a semicircle facing volunteer Judith Rastl. She triggers a lively discussion by posing questions gleaned from articles in a magazine.

"Ann," Rastl asks, "do you remember the first dance you went to? Did you go alone or did you have a date? What kind of dance did you do: the waltz, the two-step?" Ann delights in sharing her memories and soon others chime in, drawing on rich, personal experiences. Rastl passes around Edison cylinders for wind-up Victrolas and old vinyl records, and the group launches a discussion of favorite songs and music machines from the past.

Like many who perform volunteer work in Life Care centers, Rastl feels enriched by contact with the residents. "It's such a history lesson to hear these people; they lived it," she says. She finds the weekly session she leads and the preparation it requires worthwhile. "You really get close to these people," she says. "They're my friends."

Volunteers come in all ages, from teenagers working on church, school or scout projects, to elderly people who still live independently at home and enjoy assisting their peers. In the television room at Life Care Center of Scottsdale, Arizona, Mike Sullivan, 13, and 14-year-old brother, Greg, hand out warm, savory smelling bags of popcorn to residents watching a movie and clip red heart shapes for a Valentine display. The work will earn them six hours toward community service badges as members of Boy Scout Troop 649.

The Sullivans feel a personal connection to the center. "My grandfather was here two years ago when he had a stroke," Mike explains. "When I came to visit him, all the people wanted to talk to me. They told me about their jobs, where they were born." His grandfather was sent to another center. "It was awful, all messy," says Mike, a thoughtful observer. "This is the nicest nursing home I've seen. It has so many accommodations others don't have."

Many centers have a resident ambassador. It's not a formal position but one conferred by consensus, the result of a resident's desire to lift the spirits of fellow residents and staff and serve anyway possible. One resident who directed a patient escort service for Iowa Lutheran Hospital in Des Moines still spreads soothing words of comfort and assurance in her Life Care home. "She's our cheerleader," says the center's executive director.

A near-death experience during surgery motivated 92-year-old Anna Fridell to serve fellow residents at Life Care Center of Tucson. "There were people in gowns, and I was in front," she said of the vision she had. "It was very calm. We were walking and came to a line on the floor. They said, 'It's all right, Anna, you can cross over. We'll give you a push.' That's when I woke up.

"I believe I was saved to help other people," she says and has dedicated her life at the center to doing so. She visits residents, helps set tables in the dining room, presents bingo prizes, deals cards, and does whatever needs doing. She has a smile, a kind word and a loving hug for everyone.

From the monthly resident council meeting
have come ideas for the Friendship Exchange, the aviary
on the second floor, the adoption of a live-in cat, and
the annual fishing trip to the stocked lake in Idaho Springs.

Life Care Center of Evergreen, CO

Animated conversation and creative ideas arise at the monthly resident council meeting, where everyone can voice an opinion. At Life Care Center of Evergreen, west of Denver, the meeting room is full as a microphone is passed from person to person and suggestions for programs are solicited. From these discussions have come the center's Friendship Exchange, which pairs residents with children and adults in the community; the creation of an aviary on the second floor; and the adoption of a live-in cat, who prowls the halls and relishes center-stage attention.

Other major activities are assessed: the annual expedition to the stocked lake in Idaho Springs, the zany Halloween costume party, the decoration of the center's bus for the annual Evergreen Christmas parade. A debate ensues over the special meal of the month. What form of potato should accompany the entree: French fries or twice-baked? The group locks in a tie vote before the tasty issue is resolved.

Life Care fosters strong relationships between staff members and the organization and between residents and staff. "I was truly honored to be asked to work here," says Melissa Sowell, marketing director at Cottesmore of Life Care in Gig Harbor, Washington. "It feels like you're

"These people are so full of love.
They show so much courage, they ask for so little,
and they appreciate so much. You know God is looking
at all those faces and how much love He must feel."

Inez Glass
Volunteer, Cottesmore of Life Care, Gig Harbor, WA

among family. You're welcomed.

"People here believe in the mission," Sowell continues. "We're not involved with the end of life but the quality of life. Our residents recuperate so well; it's the caregiving and the atmosphere. Often people get well enough to go back home, and it's neat to be part of such a thing."

"These people are my family," says Life Care Center of Paradise Valley Executive Director Lauren Gandara of her residents. "I spend more time with them than with my own family. The majority of these people have lived a full life; they've been to war, raised families, struggled with challenges. They just need

Residents of Life Care centers are adept at savoring the moment. At Life Care Center of Colorado Springs, residents seated in wheelchairs watch a 1938, black-and-white Judy Garland film, "Listen, Darling." Garland, who plays an ingenue, sings "Zing Went The Strings Of My Heart." One resident pats her foot, and the wheels of all the chairs in the room move back and forth in unconscious synchronization to the music.

At Life Care Center of Ocala in central Florida, Amy Greene, a licensed practical nurse at the center, and resident Arthur Shuman, a retired Navy captain who commanded World War II destroyers, do their "dance." That's what Greene calls it as she expertly shifts her weight to transfer Shuman from his wheelchair to a standard cushioned chair. The decorated military leader, proud but frail, places himself in the strong arms of the nurse.

In an activity room of the center, a man in his late 60s, tanned and wearing a knit shirt and shorts, cups one hand to the mottled face of his 90-year-old mother and strokes her gray hair with the other. Her voice is thin and weak, and he bends forward to hear her speak from her wheelchair. As they talk, she clasps his hand tightly in her own.

Touch is important, a physical act of caring we never outgrow. In a sun-dappled courtyard at Life Care Center of Scottsdale, with water splashing in the pools of a three-tier fountain, a man strokes his wife's hair at the nape of her neck in a consoling way. Inside the center, short-term resident Elizabeth Reilly, learning to walk again after suffering a broken leg and a stroke, is braced at the shoulders by physical therapy assistant Martha McKeand. As Reilly practices planting her feet, McKeand's gesture speaks as much of emotional as physical support.

Sister Tonya Marie is a whirlwind of caring and good cheer, which she freely shares with residents at Life Care Center of Corona, east of Los Angeles. She flew from her convent in Guatemala to spend three weeks visiting and helping her sister, Dorothy Orland, at the center, but she doesn't confine her ministrations to her relative. She beams as she strolls the hallway, popping in to rooms to say hello to newfound friends. To one resident from her former Los Angeles parish, she gives Holy Communion. "Thanks be to God for all the gifts He gives us, yes," says Sister Tonya Marie.

Faith is a strong component of life in Life Care and never does it shine brighter than at the holiday season when associates and residents gather shoe boxes they've filled with items, from toiletries to toys, to send to children in war-torn and impoverished parts of the world. At Life Care's Cherry Hill Manor near Providence, Rhode Island, the boxes are stacked at the base of a festively adorned and lighted Christmas tree in the center's lobby. The next morning, the boxes will be placed on a truck that will begin the process of transporting Life Care's spirit of love half way around the world.

Residents demonstrate life's limitless possibilities. George and Lucille Grebert are 91 and 97 respectively and still gaze at one another with the tenderness of a newly married couple. In fact, they were 87 and 93 when they met, and they married a year later in Wellesley, Massachusetts. Now they live together at Life Care Center of Ocala in Florida.

George worked for many years for a New Jersey manufacturer and never had married. Lucille had been director of social services for New England Deaconess Hospital in Boston and enjoyed a long marriage until her husband's death. After Lucille met George, she asked him if he would go with her to Florida. He agreed only if she would marry him first. Says George: "I thought I'd be single the rest of my life." Quips Lucille: "I don't think he's made up his mind yet which is the better state, but he persisted." The two hold hands as they speak.

If variety is the spice of life, Arnold Hatfield, a resident at Mi Casa Nursing Center in Mesa, Arizona, relished it more than most. He was a contractor and inventor, a music maker and a football player, a physical therapist and a soldier, a hobo and an artist. He could fly a plane, build a mandolin, create a painting and prepare a gourmet meal.

Born into poverty in Frog Eye, Missouri, he was raised by neighbors after his mother died and his father, a sharecropper, could no longer care for him. He hopped a freight train when he was 13 so as not to financially burden others as the Depression set in. The grim life he saw crisscrossing the country (he huddled next to a man in a freezing boxcar one night to discover in the morning the man was dead) would have left many a person embittered but made him expansive. His heart grew as large as his talents, as he constantly found ways to help others, from baking bread for the needy to devising a specialized walker for a crippled friend. Now the big man is dependent on the care lavished on him by the staff.

The rhinestone tiara worn by Alice Gumm matches the sparkle in her eyes. Crowned Miss Orange Park Nursing Home Queen at the age of 100 (after flashing her legs for the judges), the lively Gumm is a repository of colorful tales. Until she was 82, she worked as a sitter caring for patients in Jacksonville, Florida, hospitals. "They just thrived over my petting," she says. Once in her early years, she delivered a young woman's baby. "It was just her and me, and I'd never done such a thing, but I knew I could," she

"In the summer, people take turns riding in the golf cart. We picnic in the orchard, eating apples and collecting material for potpourri. One resident said that with the wind and sun on her face, she hadn't felt this alive in years."

Kim Cuthbertson
Activities Director, Life Care Center of Banner Elk, NC

says, adding, "He (the baby) came to make a big, fine heavy-set man."

Gumm tackled life. As a young girl living on the St. Johns River, she hitched oxen to a yoke and drove wagons over swampy roads, took the pilot wheel of a towboat under a captain's direction and drove a lumber company train, hauling pine trees to the river to be floated to the mill. She never graduated from grammar school, but her experiences were broad. "If I'd had some education," she quips, "I might have made President."

The biographies of those who work with Life Care can be as fascinating as the residents'. Inez Glass was the youngest of 15 children. "Maybe because my mother and father were older, I always loved old people," she says. "I always felt comfortable with them."

A nurturing spirit led her to become a nurse, and in World War II, she joined the small, elite corps of flight nurses who attended wounded soldiers evacuated from the beaches of France after the D-Day invasion. After the war, she worked for nursing homes and decided to start her own. She formed a corporation that sold shares to provide the capital. Her dream facility, called Cottesmore (for the English city where she was stationed during the war), opened in Gig Harbor, Washington, in 1962. For more than 30 years she operated the highly regarded center until selling it to Life Care in 1996 when she was 76. "I always thought of us as a big family, and Life Care kept that spirit intact," she says. "I just can't say enough good about them."

But Inez Glass didn't depart the center when the purchase was made. She became the director of volunteers at Cottesmore of Life Care, bringing an uncommon dedication and a personal affiliation to her work. "These people are so full of love," she says of the residents. "They show so much courage, they ask for so little, and they appreciate so much. You know God is looking at all those faces and how much love He must feel. It just warms your heart."

A giant ferry points a snub steel bow into the gray waters of the Strait of Juan de Fuca as it rumbles from Anacortes on the northwest mainland of Washington toward Friday Harbor on San Juan Island. It threads a narrow route among mist-shrouded islands covered with firs before easing, an hour later, into the pretty harbor. Life Care's Islands Convalescent Center sits a few blocks from the water on Spring Street.

Life Care facilities are everywhere: in major cities and rural communities, in desert country and across mountain passes, from harbor towns to the heartland states, growing amid palm trees and fir trees, wherever long-term care for the elderly is needed.

But a locale like San Juan Island presents unique challenges. "We're the only nursing home in San Juan County (which covers half a dozen islands in the Strait), and there is no hospital," explains Trish

Lehman, assistant director of nursing at Islands Convalescent. "To get to a hospital in an emergency, you must either take a long ferry ride or be evacuated by helicopter. If bad weather—fog or wind—causes a power outage or keeps the ferry from running, we manage the patient, providing acute care when we have to." She adds with a smile: "We've always kind of done whatever it takes."

So do her colleagues across America. An activities assistant places the smooth face of a 71-year-old Asian resident against the lacquered face of a wooden guitar. The resident, who cannot see or hear, plucks the strings, one at a time, to feel the vibrations they make. The associate learned of this pleasure by speaking to the resident's family and spends hours each week to make certain it's delivered.

It is the appreciation of long lives lived, of wisdom gained and of the ultimate fragility of life that makes commonplace events in the halls of Life Care meaningful. A woman in a wheelchair in Florida approaches a fellow resident moving slowly with the aid of a walker. The woman in the wheelchair holds out both arms. "Give me a hug," she says with a fierce tenderness. "I love you." Her friend bends to her embrace. "I love you, too."

As sunset arrives and dinner is served and the pulse of the day starts to ebb, there are quiet moments to relish. At Scituate, Massachusetts, fishing boats return at dusk to the harbor. Gulls wheel overhead as a nurse and a resident of Life Care Center of the South Shore, located a mile from the harbor, walk a concrete path that overlooks the boats with white lights in their rigging.

At sunset on the opposite coast, a dozen residents of the Life Care Center of Vista, south of Los Angeles, gather in walkers and wheelchairs at the third-floor picture window for the evening show. As they wait, exchanging a few words of muted conversation, the fronds of two palm trees that tower outside their window grow rosy with warm color, reflecting the sun's cast as it sinks in the Pacific.

Stars burn like embers in the night sky. Charlie, the golden retriever, makes his final round. Nurse Amy Greene pirouettes with Navy Captain Shuman in their "dance" from wheelchair to bed. A soon-to-be 100-year-old operatic soprano listens, smiling, to a tape of her performance in San Antonio 65 years ago. The ferry leaves for its final run from Friday Harbor to the mainland, a carnival of lights. An associate hugs a resident, and the resident returns her embrace.

The sun rises; the sun sets - one as beautiful as the other.

Volunteer Ardee Jones plants flowers with Francis Felix on the deck of her home at Life Care Center of Tucson, AZ.

Right: Inez Glass remains a volunteer at the facility she built, operated for 34 years and sold to Life Care — Cottesmore of Life Care in Gig Harbor, WA.

Previous spread: Elaine Donovan strolls the harbor in Scituate, Massachusetts, with her father, Ben Berg, a resident of nearby Life Care Center of the South Shore, where Donovan is a nurse.

Pages 36 & 37: The lighthouse at St. Augustine stands on the Florida coast near Life Care centers in Jacksonville and Ocala.

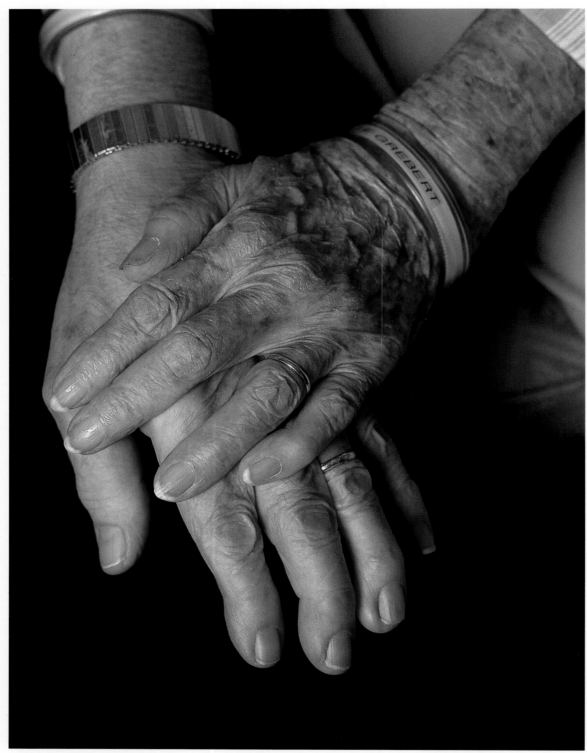

Life Care Center of Ocala, FL

Right: Married three years, the Greberts (Lucille, 97, and George, 91) reside at Life Care Center of Ocala, FL.

Previous spread: Andres Martin visits his wife, Mercedes, a resident at Garden Terrace Alzheimer's Center of Excellence in Aurora, CO.

Paul Mitchell, food services director at Life Care Center of Plymouth, has shared his talent across the country, coaching other Life Care chefs and cooking for the annual meeting.

Right: Resident and live-in greyhound, Life Care Center of Hilliard, FL

Previous spread: Sharing the day's mail is a joyful event for Marjorie Mendelsohn, left, and Anna Tegge, residents of The Bridge at Life Care Center of Ocala, FL.

Resident Beatrice Theobald enjoys the company of "Mister Tubbs" during pet day at Life Care Center of Greeneville, TN.

Hybrid wolves Kodi and Shadow are star attractions at Life Care Center of Tucson, AZ.

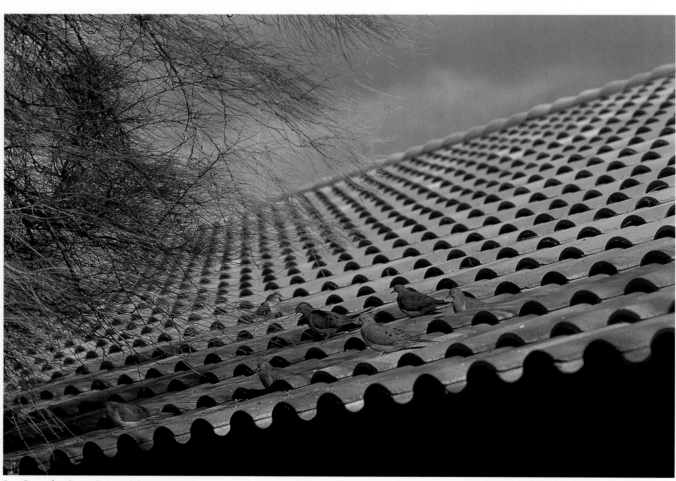

La Cañada Care Center, Tucson, AZ

Right: Traveling from a convent in Guatemala, Sister Tonya Marie visits her sister, Dorothy Orland, a resident of Life Care Center of Corona, CA.

Previous spread: An associate leads Life Care Center of Tucson residents Ann Vignola and Charles Andrews on a spirited outing at a community park.

Residents throw around their weights in the Fit For Life exercise program at Life Care Center of Nashoba Valley, Littleton, MA.

Right: Resident and therapist walk the grounds of The Bridge at Life Care Center of Ocala, FL.

Previous spread: Physical therapy assistant Martha McKeand and Elizabeth Reilly, a patient in the rehabilitation unit at Life Care Center of Scottsdale, AZ

Fit For Life exercise program, Life Care Center of Nashoba Valley, Littleton, MA

Brad Lange, director of dietary services, Life Care Center of Scottsdale, AZ

A physician makes an afternoon call, Life Care Center of Ocala, FL

Right: Certified Nursing Assistant Florence Okocha, Life Care Center of Aurora, CO

Licensed Vocational Nurse Syvonza Tucker, Rimrock Villa Convalescent Hospital, Barstow, CA

Right: Associate and resident, Rimrock Villa Convalescent Hospital, Barstow, CA

Pike's Peak is the postcard view from a hallway window at The Bridge at Life Care Center of Colorado Springs, CO.

Lobby, The Bridge at Life Care Center of Colorado Springs, CO

Enjoying the breezeway at Life Care Center of Colorado Springs, CO

Previous spread: Volunteering her time, Medical Records Coordinator Cindy Williams created a village motif for residents at Life Care Center of Hilliard, FL by making home-like entrances to their rooms.

Elegance in the private dining room at Life Care Center of Aurora, CO

Activity Director Angela Bialkowski and resident Anna Fridell, Life Care Center of Tucson, AZ

Right: Executive Director Ken Becker and resident Lora Early, Life Care Center of Greeneville, TN

The joy of activity at Life Care Center of Colorado Springs, CO

Left: Registered Nurse Sharon Batara and resident George Hartman, Life Care Center of Colorado Springs, CO

Gladys Parker, an outpatient in the sub-acute unit at La Cañada Care Center, Tucson, awaits her therapy.

Right: Life Care Center of Tucson, AZ

Previous spread: Seventy-one-year-old Kazue Matsuda, who is deaf and blind, enjoys feeling the vibrations of guitar strings with the help of
Activity Assistant Mary Ann Daley at Life Care Center of Tucson, AZ.

Resident craft, Life Care Center of Tucson, AZ

Life Care Center of Tucson, AZ

Life Care Center of Paradise Valley Glee Club, Phoenix, AZ

Right: One-hundred-year-old Alice Gumm, a resident of Life Care Center at Wells Crossing, Orange Park, FL, was crowned Miss Orange Park Nursing Home Queen.

Residents of Life Care Center of Banner Elk, NC ride their golf cart to the orchard next door.

Bouncing a beach ball on a parachute silk in a game called Body Buster is a popular physical activity at Life Care Center of Greeneville, TN.

Bingo, Life Care Center of Colorado Springs, CO

Life Care Center of Banner Elk, NC

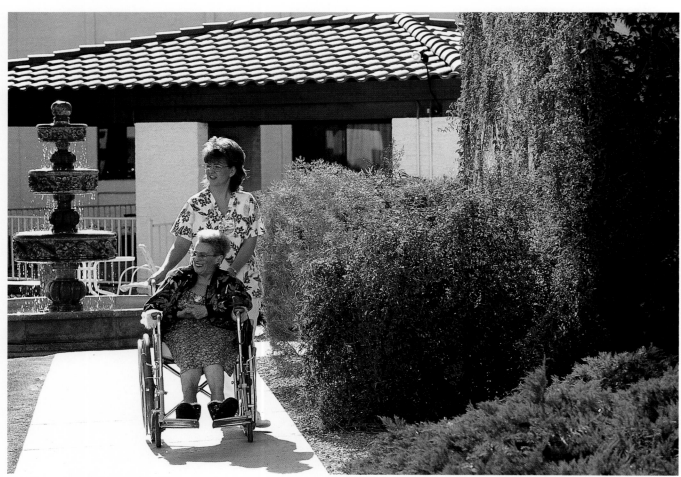

Life Care Center of Paradise Valley, Phoenix, AZ

Previous spread: Activity Director Kim Cuthbertson prepares to call numbers for eager Bingo players, Life Care Center of Banner Elk, NC

Thomas Keenan, dietary manager; his wife, LPN Kelli Keenan; and their pet, Breezy: Islands Convalescent Center, Friday Harbor, WA

a deeper speech than thou canst perceive; of ¹¹a stammering tongue, *that thou canst* not understand.

20 Look upon Zĭ'ŏn, the city of our solemnities: thine eyes shall see Jĕ-rụ'sȧ-lĕm a quiet habitation, a tabernacle *that* shall not be taken down; not one of the stakes thereof shall ever be removed, neither shall any of the cords thereof be broken.

21 But ᵏthere the glorious LORD *will be* unto us a place ¹²of broad rivers *and* streams; wherein shall go no galley with oars, neither shall gallant ship pass thereby.

22 For the LORD *is* our judge, the LORD *is* our lawgiver, ¹³'the LORD *is* our king; he will save us.

23 ¹⁴Thy tacklings are loosed; they could not well strengthen their mast, they could not spread the sail: then is the prey of a great spoil divided; the lame take the prey.

24 And the inhabitant shall not say, I am sick: ¹⁵the people that dwell therein *shall be* forgiven their iniquity.

CHAPTER 34.

1 *God's judgments upon the nations.* 11 *Desolation of all enemies.* 16 *Surety of the prophecy.*

COME near, ye nations, to hear; and hearken, ye people: let the earth hear, and all ¹ that is therein; the world, and all things that come forth of it.

2 For the indignation of the LORD *is* upon all nations, and *his* fury upon all their armies: he hath utterly destroyed them, he hath delivered them to the slaughter.

3 Their slain also shall be cast out, and their stink shall come up out of their carcases, and the mountains shall be melted with their blood.

4 And ᵃall the host of heaven shall be dissolved, and the heavens shall be rolled together as a scroll: and all their host shall fall down, as the leaf falleth off from the vine, and as a falling *fig* from the fig tree.

5 For ᵇmy sword shall be bathed in heaven: behold, it ᶜshall come down upon I-dụ-mē'ȧ, and upon the people of my curse, to judgment.

6 The sword of the LORD is filled with blood, it is made fat with fatness, *and* with the blood of lambs and goats, with the fat of the kidneys of rams: for ᵈthe LORD hath a sacrifice in Boz'rah, and a great slaughter in the land of I-dụ-mē'ȧ.

7 And the ²unicorns shall come down with them, and the bullocks with the bulls; and their land shall be ᵉsoaked with blood, and their dust made fat with fatness.

8 For *it is* the day of the LORD'S vengeance, *and* the year of recompences for the controversy of Zĭ'ŏn.

9 And the streams thereof shall be turned into pitch, and the dust thereof into brimstone, and the land thereof shall become burning pitch.

10 It shall not be quenched night nor day; the smoke thereof shall go up for ever: ᶠfrom generation to generation it shall lie waste; none shall pass through it for ever and ever.

11 ¶ But the ³cormorant and the bittern shall pos-

sess it; the owl also and the raven shall dwell in it: and he shall stretch out upon it the line of confusion, and the stones of emptiness.

12 They shall call the nobles thereof to the kingdom, but none *shall be* there, and all her princes shall be nothing.

13 And ᶠthorns shall come up in her palaces, nettles and brambles in the fortresses thereof: and it shall be an habitation of dragons, *and* a court for ⁵ ⁶owls.

14 ⁷The wild beasts of the desert shall also meet with ᵍthe wild beasts of the island, and the satyr shall cry to his fellow; the ⁹screech owl also shall rest there, and find for herself a place of rest.

15 There shall the great owl make her nest, and lay, and hatch, and gather under her shadow: there shall the vultures also be gathered, every one with her mate.

16 ¶ Seek ye out of ᵍthe book of the LORD, and read: no one of these shall fail, none shall want her mate: for my mouth it hath commanded, and his spirit it hath gathered them.

17 And he hath cast the ʰlot for them, and his hand hath divided it unto them by line: they shall possess it for ever, from generation to generation shall they dwell therein.

CHAPTER 35.

1 *Glory of the new Zion.* 8 *The way of holiness.*

THE wilderness and the solitary place shall be glad for them; and the desert shall rejoice, and blossom as the rose.

2 It shall blossom abundantly, and rejoice even with joy and singing: the glory of Lĕb'ȧ-non shall be given unto it, the excellency of Cär'mel and Shā'ron, they shall see the glory of the LORD, *and* the excellency of our God.

3 ᵃStrengthen ye the weak hands, and confirm the feeble knees.

4 Say to them *that are* of a ¹fearful heart, Be strong, fear not: behold, your God will come *with* vengeance, *even* God *with* a recompence; he will come and save you.

5 Then ᵇthe eyes of the blind shall be opened, and the ears of the deaf shall be unstopped.

6 Then shall the lame *man* leap as an hart, and the tongue of the dumb sing: for in the wilderness shall waters break out, and streams in the desert.

7 And the parched ground shall become a pool, and the thirsty land springs of water: in the habitation of dragons, where each lay, *shall be* ²grass with reeds and rushes.

8 And an highway shall be there, and a way, and it shall be called The way of holiness; ᶜthe unclean shall not pass over it; but it *shall be* for those: the wayfaring men, though fools, shall not err therein.

9 No lion shall be there, nor *any* ravenous beast shall go up thereon, it shall not be found there; but the redeemed shall walk *there*:

10 And the ransomed of the LORD shall return, and come to Zĭ'ŏn with songs and everlasting joy

man, shall devour him: but he shall flee [4] from the sword, and his young men shall be [5] discomfited.

9 And [6] he shall pass over to [7] his strong hold for fear, and his princes shall be afraid of the ensign, saith the LORD, whose *fire is* in Zī'ŏn, and his furnace in Jĕ-ru'să-lĕm.

CHAPTER 32.

1 Blessings of Christ's kingdom. 9 A prophecy of desolation. 15 The restoration promised.

BEHOLD, *a* king shall reign in righteousness, and princes shall rule in judgment.

2 And a man shall be as an hiding place from the wind, and a covert from the tempest; as rivers of water in a dry place, as the shadow of a [1] great rock in a weary land.

3 And *b* the eyes of them that see shall not be dim, and the ears of them that hear shall hearken.

4 The heart also of the [2] rash shall understand knowledge, and the tongue of the stammerers shall be ready to speak [3] plainly.

5 The vile person shall be no more called liberal, nor the churl said *to be* bountiful.

6 For the vile person will speak villany, and his heart will work iniquity, to practise hypocrisy, and to utter error against the LORD, to make empty the soul of the hungry, and he will cause the drink of the thirsty to fail.

7 The instruments also of the churl *are* evil: he deviseth wicked devices to destroy the poor with lying words, even [4] when the needy speaketh right.

8 But the liberal deviseth liberal things; and by liberal things shall he [5] stand.

9 ¶ Rise up, ye women *that are* at ease; hear my voice, ye careless daughters; give ear unto my speech.

10 [6] Many days and years shall ye be troubled, ye careless women: for the vintage shall fail, the gathering shall not come.

11 Tremble, ye women that are at ease; be troubled, ye careless ones: strip you, and make you bare, and gird *sackcloth* upon *your* loins.

12 They shall lament for the teats, for [7] the pleasant fields, for the fruitful vine.

13 *a* Upon the land of my people shall come up thorns *and* briers; [8] yea, upon all the houses of joy in the joyous city:

14 Because the palaces shall be forsaken; the multitude of the city shall be left; the [9] forts and towers shall be for dens for ever, a joy of wild asses, a pasture of flocks;

15 Until *e* the spirit be poured upon us from on high, and the wilderness be a fruitful field, and the fruitful field be counted for a forest.

16 *f* Then judgment shall dwell in the wilderness, and righteousness remain in the fruitful field.

17 *g* And the work of righteousness shall be peace; and the effect of righteousness quietness and assurance for ever.

18 And my people shall dwell in a peaceable habitation, and in sure dwellings, and in quiet resting places;

508

19 When it shall hail, coming down *h* on the forest; [10] and the city shall be low in a low place.

20 Blessed *are* ye that sow beside all waters, that send forth *thither* the feet of *i* the ox and the ass.

CHAPTER 33.

1 Judgments against the church's enemies. 13 The godly are privileged.

WOE to thee *a* that spoilest, and thou *wast* not spoiled; and dealest treacherously, and they dealt not treacherously with thee! *b* when thou shalt cease to spoil, thou shalt be spoiled; *and* when thou shalt make an end to deal treacherously, they shall deal treacherously with thee.

2 O LORD, be gracious unto us; we have waited for thee: be thou their arm every morning, our salvation also in the time of trouble.

3 At the noise of the tumult the people fled; at the lifting up of thyself the nations were scattered.

4 And your spoil shall be gathered *like* the gathering of the caterpiller: as the running to and fro of locusts shall he run upon them.

5 *c* The LORD is exalted; for he dwelleth on high: he hath filled Zī'ŏn with judgment and righteousness.

6 *d* And wisdom and knowledge shall be the stability of thy times, *and* strength of [1] salvation: the fear of the LORD *is* his treasure.

7 Behold, their [2] valiant ones s... the ambassad...

8 *f* The high... peace shall... ceaseth: he... e waste, the... spised the cit...

9 The earth... aken the c... is ashamed... egardeth... derness; an... th *and* la... fruits...

10 ... n down... ex... n and... no... shall... y... th...

Center column notes:

4 Or, for fear of the sword.
5 for melting, or, tributary.
6 his rock shall pass away for fear.
7 Or, his strength.
ι Lev. 6. 13.

1 heavy.
b ch. 29. 18.
2 hasty.
3 Or, elegantly.
4 Or, when he speaketh against the poor in judgment.
5 be established.
e Amos 6. 1.
6 Days above a year.
7 the fields of desire.
d Hos. 9. 6.
8 Or, burning upon, etc.
9 Or, clifts and watchtowers.
e Ps. 104. 30.
f Zech. 8. 3.
g Jam. 4. 2, 3. Mic. 4. 4, 5. Luke 2. 1. 3.
h Zech. 11. 2.
10 Or, and the city shall be utterly abased.
i ch. 30. 24.

Right column notes:

a Hab. 2. 8.
b Rev. 13. 10.
c Ps. 97. 9.
d Prov. 1. 7.
1 Matt. 6. 33.
2 Or, messengers.

... defence
... d shall be
... n his beauty:
... ery far off.
... rror. 'Where *is*
... ver? where *is* he
... people, *ja* people of

Stained glass window, Life Care Center of Evergreen, CO

Right: Courtyard, Life Care Center of Corona, CA

Previous spread: Resident Olive Allen's family Bible, Life Care Center of Elizabethton, TN

Santa, resident and child, Life Care Center of Morristown, TN

Right: The spirit of a Life Care Christmas, Cherry Hill Manor Nursing Home, Johnston, RI

Previous spread: Assistant Director of Nursing Dawn Gonnelli, left, and Activity Director Grace Horton wrap Operation Christmas Child
  gifts at Cherry Hill Manor Nursing Home, Johnston, RI.
Following spread: December sunset, Life Care Center of Escondido, CA

Treasure Portraits

Public notables and everyday heroes
reside in Life Care centers across America. Whether
they acted their part on the large stage or small in the
course of their years matters not; they enriched the lives
of those around them.

These profiles represent the thousands of inspiring
stories from Life Care that form a treasured tapestry. Each
is worthy of the telling.

THE MUSIC MAN

Joseph Wright: Big-Band Pianist

From culturally parched hinterlands to big-city emporiums, through eras of economic hardship and rollicking affluence, from the standards of Gershwin to the hits of Presley, Joseph Wright played.

He played on giant Wurlitzer organs and small upright pianos. He played at movie houses before there were talkies and for midnight theater sing-alongs. He played for churches, and he played in lounges, where a few bars hummed were all he needed to fill out a tune.

He played with big-name bands like Whiteman and Welk, directed the music for exotic fan-dancer Sally Rand, and worked for MGM studios in California, transcribing notes for movie scores alongside a cadre of musical geniuses who'd fled Nazi Europe. And wherever Wright played, people smiled.

He began playing in Fort Worth, Texas. His father, a plumber, wanted his only boy to take up the trade, but his mother, an artist, seemed to prevail. As an eight-year-old, Wright began

piano lessons with an aunt, then studied with the classically trained musician, Dr. Carl Venth, former concert master for New York's Metropolitan Opera, who had moved to Fort Worth in the latter stage of his career.

Ironically, though, it was Wright's father who shoved him into performing. In 1924, the elder Wright was president of the National Association of Plumbers and Steamfitters, which was holding its annual convention in Dallas. When an entertainer for an afternoon session failed to show, he asked his son to play for 2,400 restless attendees. The father never waited for a response. With a kick in the pants, he propelled the 13-year-old on stage.

"I couldn't run," says Wright. "There was nothing to do but sit down and play. I was trembling like a leaf, but as soon as I began, the fear went away." Four joyful encores of "The Merry Widow's Waltz" ensued, and that "took the fear of audiences out of me forever."

Soon began life on the road. Hired by Paramount, he traveled its theater circuit, accompanying silent films. He joined the big bands during the Depression, playing a fill-in role with Lawrence Welk and as a regular in the popular Paul Whiteman band. He later met George Gershwin and other music and theater notables while working at MGM.

In later life, Wright taught over 200 pupils. He was "beloved organist" for a Seventh-day Adventist Church and played 18 years, at no charge, for a senior luncheon program in Gardena, California.

In the lobby of Life Care's assisted living center in Corona, he plays the "Twelfth Street Rag" on a 75-year-old upright. It's his twice weekly after-dinner treat for fellow residents. His long fingers attack the keys with gusto, and, his listeners, as they have for 80 years, tap their toes and smile.

Joseph Wright, 88, Corona Crest Assisted Living Center, Corona, California

A TRIBUTE TO HER LAND

Carmen Beltran: *Mexican Culturist*

Growing up in Durango, Mexico, where she was born in 1905, Carmen Celia Beltran basked in the arts. Her father owned a music store and led classical ensembles. Her mother played mandolin and sang. One brother was a trombonist; another a concert violinist. Family friends were authors and composers. As a child, Carmen played piano and wrote poems and plays.

Then came the tumultuous years of Pancho Villa and the Mexican revolution. "There was so much grief and sorrow," she recalls. The upheaval deepened her love for her native country even as it drove her family into political exile in the United States. As an honor student and budding actress at a San Antonio, Texas, high school in the early 1920s, her course was already set. She would devote her life to the arts in the name of the country she loved.

Beltran moved to Los Angeles to join its vibrant live-theater community, where she gained acclaim as an actress, dancer, playwright and poet who worked in her native Spanish and promoted Mexican culture at every turn. She carried that reputation to Tucson, Arizona, where she moved in 1938. Adding Mexican history and music to her repertoire, she became a spokesperson for the heritage of her homeland and a cultural bridge for those who had left Mexico, whether months or generations ago.

After decades of writing and producing plays in Tucson and making guest appearances on radio shows, Beltran was given a 45-minute program of her own on Tucson's public radio station, KUAT. In 1981, "Homenaje a la Musica Mexicana" (A Tribute to Mexican Music) debuted. Airing Sunday after-

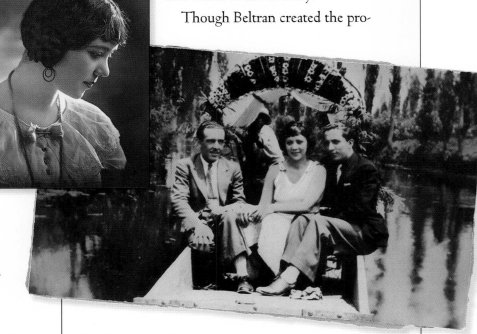

noons, it featured thematic programs, from female composers to music of the regions — all in high cultural style. No ranchero music was played unless soft and melodic and "never mariachi," Beltran says emphatically. Woven into her commentary was discussion of the history and values of the country.

Though Beltran created the program's last installment in 1985, so well produced is the series that it continues in rebroadcasts on Sundays in Tucson. It's now part of a legacy that includes such plays as "The Empty Cradle," telling a story of war's personal toll, her books of poetry, and her community projects that celebrate Mexican history and heritage.

Recipient of community, state and regional honors including the Pan American Theatrical Association's Cesar Award, she retains a proud bearing and a passion for Mexican culture. "I think everything in life comes because it has to," she says of her work. "I was following my natural interests."

In so doing, she built a bridge made of art that many gratefully cross to this day.

Carmen Beltran, 94, LaCañada Care Center, Tucson, Arizona

HAVING THE FINAL WORD

Alfred E. Smith: *Big Sur Essayist*

As long as Alfred E. Smith can remember, he dreamed of writing. "I wanted to from childhood," he says. His passion for the written word led him to literature studies at Yale University and to lively letters, more like discourses, penned to friends. Later, that passion found an outlet in copy written for his clients at a San Francisco advertising agency.

Eventually it drew him to Big Sur, California, and the artist colony of Carmel, where he served on the foundation that oversaw the estate of the late poet Robinson Jeffers and where he rubbed shoulders with creative spirits, from photographer Ansel Adams to actor Clint Eastwood.

But it wasn't until he had 84 years of rich, sometimes poignant, often humorous life experience under his belt that his secret ambition took wing. He published a collection of essays under the title: *TAKE ONE AT BEDTIME: Forty-four Beguiling Tales about Carmel, Birds, and Paper Airplanes.* "I didn't know how much fun it was to be an author and have your book selling," says the handsome, white-maned Smith. The writer in him was loose.

The book marked his fourth career. The first, as a teacher of college English, lasted but six months. He had received a master's degree in literature from Yale, but despite those impressive credentials, the classroom wasn't to be home. He says, with understatement: "A professor took me aside and said I might do better in a different line of work."

That work would involve "the mystic world of advertising," as he calls it, and his tenure would be longer: 25 years. At a large San Francisco agency he found variety and excitement, if not the calling of teaching he was seeking, working with a roster of national clients, from Gallo Wine to Clorox Bleach.

He retired from the agency — for three days — before launching career number three, as a consultant. For seven years, he assisted the management of a large electrical firm to make it profitable and grow. Meanwhile, he and his family moved to Carmel, south of San Francisco on the Pacific coast, where they enjoyed some of America's most stimulating company and dramatic scenery.

The Carmel days enliven his book. He recounts memorable experiences at the family's mountainside home, weighs in with humorous observations of human nature and profiles eccentric characters in the neighborhood.

The book also describes a romantic miracle in his life. In 1936, on a United Airlines flight, Smith, a 22-year-old Yale-bound student, met stewardess Hazel French. It was affection at first sight. Over the next three years, they met as their schedules permitted, on one magical New York night dancing to Tommy Dorsey's live band and taking a serenaded carriage ride in Central Park.

The two, however, married other people and moved to opposite ends of the country. Then, after 50 years, when their long marriages had ended in the death of their spouses, and through a series of chance events, they found each other again. The reunion culminated in a catered party at his Carmel home attended by 50 family members and friends.

"We announced our engagement — for life," Smith tells his readers with relish. "At our age," he adds, "it's perfect." And engaged they've remained ever since.

Alfred E. Smith, 85, Life Care Center of Ocala, Florida

MAKE A JOYFUL SOUND

Agnes Benagh: *Operatic Soprano*

It was a gift, a three-and-a-half-octave marvel of soprano range and feeling, that Agnes Benagh showered on audiences of operagoers and church worshipers, bedridden babies and homesick GIs.

She sang for troops, for churches, for children's hospitals — for "anyone who wanted me," she says. It was her purpose in life. And she never took a dime for a performance. "God gave it to me," she declares of a voice pure as a flute, ornamented with the trills and runs of a coloratura. "I've always sung for God."

The instrument she used so freely was cultivated in a musical family in Bryan, Texas. Her mother, a singer, encouraged Benagh and her nine sisters to play piano and sing. Her father, a physician and hospital director, insisted the self-confident Benagh (pronounced BAY-nuh) receive voice lessons from the finest teachers he could find, including former Metropolitan Opera performers.

"Come in here, Miss Priss, and I'll see what you can do," said one instructor for whom Benagh, projecting a bit of cockiness, was to audition. "He tried to get me off key but couldn't," she proudly recalls.

Benagh's prodigious gift showed itself early. At age five, she was lifted to a tabletop covered with rose petals to perform before a crowded Bryan theater. Her voice possessed not only range (she was compared to famed soprano Jenny Lind, the "Swedish Nightingale," who enthralled American audiences and whose folk songs were in Benagh's repertoire) but longevity. Benagh was singing on a Canadian concert tour at the age of 94.

She attended college in Houston on a voice scholarship. In 1926, she married John Simmons, an engineer and attorney who served in the Army's Judge Advocate Corps. The couple moved to Washington, D.C. where Benagh appeared in concerts and served on the board of the Washington Opera Guild. Invited to join New York City's Metropolitan Opera when she was 30, she declined, refusing to take the time from her husband and two-year-old son.

Her singing continued, always for free. During the Second World War, she joined a Red Cross show that toured American Army bases where soldiers were training for overseas duty. From Mozart's "Hallelujah" to black spirituals, she moved her young, homesick audiences.

The family later moved to San Antonio, Texas. After the death of her first husband, she married Maclin Benagh, an engineer who had helped build the Panama Canal. "Maclin saw the wedding of the waters of the Gulf and Pacific," she says with delight. Benagh formed her own company that performed popular arias for civic and school groups. For 40 years, she entertained children at a pediatric hospital in San Antonio. "I saw them die," she says of the patients, "but I also saw them get well and get married."

Regarding her voice as a divine gift, she found it most joyous to sing in church, where she replaced tragic arias with hymns of hope and faith. When someone asked to record her while she sang in a service, Benagh refused. "I didn't want anything mechanical in the church because I was singing from my soul," she says. "I was singing for God."

Agnes Benagh, 99, Marysville Care Center, Marysville, Washington

PROVIDING LIFE'S STAPLES

Blair King: Island Grocer

To the farmers and fishermen of the San Juan Islands in the vast Straits of Juan de Fuca at the northwest tip of Washington state, King's Market on Spring Street, in the islands' main port of Friday Harbor, shone fair as a lighthouse beacon on a stormy day.

The family grocery run by Blair King and his wife, Viola (Vi, as she's called), was more than a supermarket that stocked the staples needed by residents who lived an hour's ferry ride from the mainland. It offered the helping hand those isolated on an island sometimes need to survive.

After a full, five-day work week, the Kings were open Saturday nights so farmers could come to town and place their weekly orders and Sunday afternoons so seine boat captains could take on provisions before heading to sea. If boats were driven back to harbor at two in the morning, the Kings were there to bring them supplies. Small, neighboring islands relied on the Kings for their weekly groceries. Blair cut the meat, Vi collected the dry goods and the order was boxed up for the boat that was sent.

To ease the vagaries of life on the San Juan Islands, the Kings would carry charge accounts for farmers for a year until their lambs and crops were sold and wait a season for full payment from fishermen until their catch was bought by the cannery. To assist the community's elderly shut-ins, the Kings made personal grocery deliveries every Friday.

When the Kings heard of a family in distress, they helped. "People tell me how Mom and Dad took care of their needs when they were struggling," says son, Rick, who worked at the market. "They would help a woman with staples while her husband fished, then would accept the fish as a token payment. On the island," he adds, "people basically take care of one another."

Blair King worked for his father, Lyle, who started the market in 1929, and purchased the business in 1948 upon his father's death. Blair and Vi ran the store until 1979 when they sold it to a mainlander who retained the popular "King's Market" name. With so much of his life invested in the store, Blair King continued to work at it each day, at no pay. "I still went in," he says of his early morning arrivals to welcome delivery men. "These were the things I wanted to do."

There were other things he did that earned the respect and affection of neighbors. He was a town councilman, chamber of commerce director, bank board member and grand marshal of the July Fourth parade. Vi was a leader in the 4-H Girls Club and the PTA and involved in other school functions.

And there were countless unofficial acts of kindness bestowed by the Kings. They would give young people pick-up work so they'd have money. "Dad would be told of a family of four with no money," says his daughter, Susan. "He'd tell them to take a shopping cart and fill it up. There'd be no charge."

"Mom and Dad did everything together," says Rick. "Their whole life was their children, their store and their community." Thanks to the Kings, life on the islands was sweeter.

Blair King, 88, Islands Convalescent Center, Friday Harbor, Washington

AN ARTFUL LIFE

Maria Holmes: Portraitist/Dancer

Maria Breidenbach Holmes lived in a world brilliant with color and music and movement. She painted life-size, prize-winning portraits (her showings included the Smithsonian) and played classical keyboard compositions. She appeared on stage (once with a young Robert Duvall), and danced in elaborate ballroom gowns she made herself.

She drove bright red cars and wore flowing, lace-edged dresses and a full red wig always topped with a clip or bow — a swirl of color and elegance wherever she went. She was an artist in fact and in attitude: animated, dramatic, temperamental, irrepressible, quirky, humorous. To enter her arc was to feel the creative spark.

Holmes was born in 1914 in Dayton, Ohio, and graduated from Dayton Art Institute. She received early recognition, winning juried competitions and receiving portrait commissions.

While painting was the central interest of her artistic life, music and ballroom dancing were close behind. She was proficient in piano and accordion and accompanied husband Leonard Holmes, a part-time operatic baritone. On occasion, she took the stage, once appearing in a workshop performance of "Madame Butterfly" sponsored by the Metropolitan Opera.

Dance was a recreational interest she pursued with the same fervor and delight as all her endeavors. From flamingo to ballroom to swing, she and her partners would participate in "showcase" events. She brought to the floor not only a flair for movement but design, creating and sewing her dresses, fashioning simple materials into beautiful gowns.

She insisted her son and daughter learn to play musical instruments and later tried, unsuccessfully, to lead her son and daughter-in-law into ballroom dancing. She loved to sew for her family and to play piano for them, as she did for her congregation's Children's Church on Sundays.

Non-conformity was her hallmark. The oven of her apartment was filled not with food (she didn't like to cook) but oil paints, and the second bathroom was a closet for canvases. So immersed was she in the world of art that she failed to notice an urban riot underway in Baltimore where she was living in the 1960s. When no one ventured out, she calmly went, asking a milling group of men the way to an art supply store, receiving directions and leaving unbothered, unhurt and unaware.

Her talent isn't lost on her family. Her daughter, Daryle, is a painter and actress. Her son, Ward, designs and builds commercial products. The grandchildren possess creative gifts. "Her imagination and creativity are passed down," says her son. So, it's hoped, is a sense of humor retained by the matriarch, whose incandescent nature brightens the world.

Maria Holmes, 85, Life Care Center at Wells Crossing, Orange Park, Florida

TALL IN THE SADDLE

Lonnie Arrington: *Horse Trainer*

Lonnie "Pock" Arrington is the adult stuff of children's dreams: a rawboned, cantankerous, lovable man who's had in his lifetime more and, to hear him tell it, finer conversations with horses than people, but who has loved nothing better than swinging a kid into the saddle for the first time and teaching the responsibility of caring for a mount.

Arrington grew up with horses on a farm in Missouri: big Belgian draft horses, "good old cow ponies," horses that pulled wagons and horses bred for trick riding. He even cared for his grandfather's buffalo, "Old Grunter." If it could be led or ridden, Pock Arrington would take the reins.

He moved to Colorado where he didn't keep the love of horses to himself. He ran a stable for many years, did television and newspaper promotions with a horse-drawn wagon (he used a Conestoga for a Studebaker ad), and drove hay wagons pulled by draft horses for children's parties.

His reputation among professional riders was considerable. "Whenever Dick Griffith (world champion bull and trick rider from Scottsdale, Arizona) came to Colorado, he always boarded his horses with me," Arrington notes proudly. They knew that Arrington put the horses first. "They even ate before I did," he says with a laugh. And nothing kept him from his rounds. When the inevitable injury occurred — a broken collar bone, one time — he kept right on working. "Never drew a day of unemployment," he says.

Most will say the finest thing Arrington did was put children where he loved to be — astride a horse. To this end, he helped found the Westernaires, a riding club that spread its chapters across Colorado. Youngsters who'd never seen the world from a horse's back were awe-struck by the feeling, and the view. Arrington carried them from the rudiments of horsemanship to trick riding. Eventually, they performed in public, as synchronized riders at rodeos and other Western-style events.

"He taught me to ride and take care of horses, and he taught the responsibility of caring for horses to numerous kids," says granddaughter Cherie Mazurek. "He always had time for kids; he was there for them," she adds. They returned the affection, calling the tough, wiry man, "Pocky," and throwing neighborhood birthday parties for him.

The community, too, bestowed its recognition. For his years of service to youngsters through the Westernaires and local Willowbrook stable he owned and managed, Arrington Park in Jefferson County near Denver was named in his honor.

In a television interview he once gave, Arrington was his crusty best. He asserted that horses were better than humans. "They don't talk back to you, and they appreciate every damn thing you do for them," he declared. Asked about the physical work he was still performing in his late 80s, he quipped: "I've worn out two sets of horses, three pickups and one pair of legs."

Friends say it's his heart that stays forever young.

Lonnie Arrington, 92, Life Care Center of Evergreen, Colorado

FIRST IN HER CLASS

Frances "Jim" Wright: *Yellowstone Ranger*

In 1926, when she first put on a National Park Service uniform (specially tailored for a woman) and began welcoming visitors to the north entrance of Yellowstone, 19-year-old Frances Wright became an American original: the country's first female ranger.

No one was better suited to take the step. She had moved with her family to Yellowstone in 1915, at age eight, when her father, Thad Pound, became a scout at the U.S. Army fort located there. When the National Park Service was created the following year, Pound was mustered in as one of the Service's original Yellowstone rangers.

The park became Wright's playground. She learned to ski from an Army scout, who later became Yellowstone's chief ranger. She joined her father on boundary patrol on horseback and fed elk and buffalo in the harsh winters. Her yen for physical adventure and tomboy ways earned her the nickname "Jim," after a popular, Dennis-the-Menace-type cartoon character of the day.

The name helped her land the ranger's job. Aware of her experience, Yellowstone Superintendent Horace Albright asked if she'd like to be a ranger. He explained that a woman had never been hired for the post, and to avoid a gender stir, he wanted to use her nickname on the application. "Jim" Pound was hired, no questions asked.

Her job included registering visitors at the Roosevelt Arch north entrance, sealing guns with lead plugs so they couldn't be fired in Yellowstone, providing park information, helping care for injured and abandoned animals, and enforcing park rules, which led to her arresting several bootleggers.

The perky young woman with a man's name and job caught the eye of the national press. *The New York Sun*, among others, ran her picture above the caption:

"They call her Ranger Jim."

The park service job ended in 1929. "Jim" married, became a mother, worked as a secretary and taught Red Cross first-aid classes to everyone: work colleagues, police departments, PTA clubs and scout troops.

But her Park Service exploits weren't forgotten. At the 75th anniversary of the Service in 1991, she was presented one of ten replicas of the original ranger badge. For Yellowstone's 125th anniversary in 1997, she was an honored guest and speaker. While there, she donated her original uniform to the Museum of the National Park Ranger.

Four years are a thin slice of a long life, but they marked her forever. "People had never heard such a thing at the time — a woman as a ranger," says Wright. "You feel quite proud to be regarded as having done something that different."

Frances Wright, 92, Life Care Center of San Gabriel, California

WORTH HIS SALT

Edwin Shuman, Jr.: Destroyer Captain

He stood before the masts of America's fastest schooners and the cannons of its powerful destroyers. In peace and in war, the hope of victory rested on his shoulders.

Edwin Arthur Shuman, Jr., naval architect, celebrated yachtsman, U.S. Navy captain, carried that responsibility with an easy, Yankee grace.

The Boston native and Georgetown University graduate began his career as a yacht designer and racer. He competed for the United States against Sweden and Germany and sailed on the crew that held a 24-year speed record in the Bermuda Ocean Race. He later designed a yacht that won the Canada Cup.

A year before America's entry in World War II, he enlisted in the Navy and was commissioned a lieutenant junior grade. At Boston Naval Yard, he switched from building sleek racing hulls to supervising construction of mine sweepers, submarine chasers, diving tenders

and PT boats.

Soon he was commanding a patrol craft and, a year later, the U.S.S. Laning, a destroyer escort working in Atlantic, Mediterranean and African waters. Before the war's end, he would be commended for action off the North African coast and have taken part in the occupations of Korea and China.

Between 1945 and 1950, he commanded four Navy destroyers and participated in the atomic bomb test at Bikini Island. He then began a stint as a navigation instructor at the Naval Academy in Annapolis.

Racing never left his blood. In 1952, he was named vice commodore of the Naval Academy's sailing squadron and that year skippered the Highland Light in the Bermuda Ocean Race, an event he won 11 years later.

More Navy adventure lay ahead. He joined the command staff of the U.S. Sixth Fleet and moved his family to the south of France. "They followed the ships," he says. "It was a great life."

In 1960, he commanded the U.S.S. Arneb in "Operation Deep Freeze" to Antarctica to permanently close Admiral Byrd's station. Directors of the National Science Foundation and field workers, from scientists to a watercolorist, were aboard.

A year later the family moved to Turkey where he'd been posted as American advisor to that country's navy. "They loved him; they called him the Big Pasha," says his daughter, Sally Smyth. "My father never does things half way; that's not his style. He just takes a situation and turns it shipshape so fast. He's a Bostonian and a Pilgrim."

Years after retirement from the Navy and racing, he still hears from men who served under his command. "He was tough, but he was liked," says Smyth. "The chiefs and young sailors still write."

Edwin Shuman, Jr., 93, Life Care Center of Ocala, Florida

HOLDING NEW LIFE

Anoise Wainwright: Obstetrical Nurse

Anoise Wainwright never tallied how many babies she helped bring into the world. Let's see: thirty years as a registered nurse in the labor-and-delivery suite at St. Vincent's Hospital in Jacksonville, Florida. As many as 11 deliveries on a shift.

A lot.

"I've run into mothers on the street," says the retired nurse, who wears the beatific smile of one who has witnessed profoundly joyful events. "They'll say, 'Oh, Miss Wainwright, don't you remember me? You were with me when I delivered my baby.' Many times, I don't remember them at all, but it's nice to know you played such an important role in their life that they never forgot you."

She came to her calling by twists and turns. An older brother paid Wainwright's tuition to St. Vincent's nursing school, enabling her to fulfill a childhood dream and, incidentally, join three first cousins in the profession. But the study of obstetrics wasn't her strength. In fact, she flunked that portion of her registered nursing exam, requiring her to re-take the test.

Distraught by her failure, she told Sister Mary Clare, a young St. Vincent's nun, that she was quitting. "Sister said, 'No you're not!' and hired me a tutor. I passed, and nursing became a part of my life that I wouldn't trade for anything. I loved it, and I loved OB (obstetrics)."

How did she come to that specialty? The hospital was short one nurse in the labor and delivery department during a shift, and Wainwright, who had been caring for general medical and surgical patients, was asked by a nun to fill in. "I was afraid I wouldn't know what to do, but Sister told me to just help out and see how it went."

The joy of childbirth was, for Wainwright, a transporting experience. "I never left. I loved all the excitement of the mothers and babies. I went hog wild."

She assisted with normal deliveries and scrubbed for surgical Caeserean sections when a physician couldn't be found quickly enough. After deliveries, she prepared infants for the nursery, banding and fingerprinting them and treating their eyes. "We made sure mothers and babies were clearly identified," she says. "I don't know how babies ever get switched by mistake."

She encountered religious prejudice when some acquaintances learned she was working at the city's Catholic hospital, a place that became her second home. "People said, 'They'll want to make you a Catholic.' I said, 'That's bull.' You hear a lot of brainless things."

She did become Catholic, in the broad sense. "Before we went on duty, my roommate and I would always go by the chapel to pray to the Good Lord to see all my patients through the night," she says. During those silent petitions for support uttered amid the icons of the church, she says, "I was a Baptist, but a Catholic, too."

Anoise Wainwright never had children of her own, but the thousands she helped bring into the world, and the four nieces and nephews she dotes on, are stunning compensation. "I didn't lack for anything," she says. "I had all the babies I wanted."

Anoise Wainwright, 72, Life Care Center of Hilliard, Florida

A GIFT TO NEWLAND

Raymond Ford: Small-Town Mayor

After serving as a pay clerk attached to Eisenhower's command in World War II and then building a successful career with finance companies in the South, Raymond Ford was ready for retirement. He and his wife, Ella, traded the big-city pace of Atlanta for her small hometown of Newland, perched 3,600 feet high in the Blue Ridge Mountains of western North Carolina.

But instead of becoming a sleepy address for Ford, Newland would launch his late-life career. Setting events in motion was the felony conviction of Newland's mayor for attempting to bribe a patrolman who'd arrested him for driving under the influence.

The mayor was sentenced to a year in jail, leaving the city's top post vacant. Ford's brother-in-law, who was sheriff of Avery County, which Newland serves as county seat, suggested to the governor's office that the most capable person in town to complete the term was retiree Raymond Ford.

Ford did offer impressive credentials. A graduate of the Army's finance school, he was assigned to payroll operations in England, Algeria and Italy during the war. He saw Generals Clark and Patton (with his jeep horn blaring) call on Eisenhower, and, on one occasion, says Ford, in his down-home style: "Me and this old boy went to the Bank of England and counted out the invasion money for the troops."

By comparison, counting Newland's (pop. 500) tiny city payroll would be a breeze. Ford could also count on years of working with loan documents for finance companies to help him master the intricacies of applying for state and federal municipal grants. Governor Jim Hunt appointed Ford to serve the remaining year of the mayor's term.

The town took quickly to Ford, who subsequently won election to four two-year terms, rejuvenating Newland in the process. He procured grants to enlarge the police force from one officer patrolling in a beat-up Chrysler to four officers in cruisers providing 24-hour surveillance. He wrested $400,000 in government grants to build a sewer plant, purchased trucks for the maintenance department and paved Main Street for the first time in 13 years.

He also tackled residents who wouldn't pay their taxes. One man, who hadn't paid in years, possessed a good job, nice house, late model car, boat and bank account. "Sonny," he told Ford, "I've never paid taxes, and I'm not going to start this late in life." But when he learned Ford was planning to attach his assets, he was at City Hall the next afternoon, paying the delinquent taxes with penalty interest. Yet, to another resident who lived on a meager monthly Social Security payment, Ford vowed: "Hon, as long as I'm mayor, you'll never pay a penny of tax."

"It was a great experience," says Ford of his days in Newland. For the town, it was a boon. "He was always working to get grants for the town and see it progress," says former *Avery Journal* Editor Bertie Burleson. "He made us into a finer place to live."

Raymond Ford, 82, Life Care Center of Banner Elk, North Carolina

FAITH GOES TO WAR

Olive Allen: Asian-field Missionary

The diminutive teacher with twinkling eyes and a Southern drawl lived with spies in her midst and saw bombs light the sky at night. But neither guerrillas nor air attacks could deter Olive Allen from her rounds, teaching English, often through Bible songs and verses, to kindergartners in war-ravaged Southeast Asia.

With a disarming gentleness and a bedrock faith, this Baptist missionary from the hills of Tennessee gathered small Thai and Vietnamese children around her in classrooms in the 1960s and '70s when chaos and death rocked their world. She brought learning, moments of gaiety, and a message of hope that life would improve.

"I knew they were having such a hard time; they had hardly anyone teaching in the villages," she says. "I loved to work with the children, and the parents loved you for working with them."

Raised in the East Tennessee hamlet of Siam ("When I went to Thailand, I told them: 'I'm from Siam; I'm Siamese, too,'" she says with a laugh), Allen knew she wanted to be an educator but yearned for more than secular schools could offer. The religious life beckoned, and in 1948, she answered the call to become a foreign missionary. "I had to turn loose and go where I was needed," she says.

Armed with a teaching degree and graduate studies at Columbia University, she embarked for the Hawaiian island of Oahu on the heels of the Second World War to teach kindergarten-age children of many nationalities. "The parents wanted their children to be educated in the American style and were glad to get an English-speaking teacher," she says.

When Hawaii became a U.S. territory and was no longer deemed a foreign mission, she took her church-sponsored work to Thailand. Southeast Asia was then a tinderbox; neighboring Laos was on the verge of collapse and Vietnam was at war.

Olive Allen was at peace. "My real purpose was to spread the Bible and Christianity," she says. Along the way, she spread a liberal dose of education, opening kindergartens in the country. She later moved to Vietnam, where spies and danger lurked. One young man, who turned out to be a spy, so ingratiated himself in her community that she still marvels at how "tactfully" he did his work.

Her own work blossomed. Children learned English and the Bible's core values. Some of her students eventually entered universities and the ministry. When forced to leave South Vietnam prior to its fall, she volunteered to work with Vietnamese boat people at the refugee center at Fort Chaffee, Arkansas.

Olive Allen fondly remembers her children marching in for the annual Christmas program, each with a candle, and their delight in singing while holding their small Bibles in the air. "I wish I could go back," she says, wistfully, then in a small but lively voice sings a favorite rhyme she taught her students: "B-I-B-L-E; Oh, that's the book for me. I stand alone, on the word of God; the B-I-B-L-E."

From the look on her face, Olive Allen has returned.

Olive Allen at one of her mission schools

Olive Allen, 93, Life Care Center of Elizabethton, Tennessee

"YOU CAN WAKE THEM UP"

Gary Helsing: *Vietnam Vet*

In the early 1970s, Gary Helsing served back-to-back tours of duty in Vietnam. Yet, the greatest battle of his life lay ahead.

By 1982, the burly veteran with a tattooed snake on his forearm and a case of Vietnam medals above his bed was no longer in the Navy, where he planned to spend a career, but confined to a wheelchair in a nursing home, where multiple sclerosis and muscular dystrophy brought him.

He was the age of fellow residents' grandchildren when he began living in the first of several facilities before finding his way to Life Care. But instead of feeling life was over at 31, Helsing determined to make a difference.

He became a life member of Paralyzed Veterans of America (PVA), helping the organization lobby Congress for greater accessibility to building and stores. "We wrote the first disability act and came up with the design of the handicap parking symbol," he says proudly.

He helped start a VFW post and helped organize a welcome-home parade for Vietnam vets in Chicago, using his computer bulletin board to spread word of the event nationwide.

He won medals in Special Olympics events and toured the White House, where he met President Reagan. That occurred when Helsing traveled to Washington for a memorial service at the Vietnam Wall and received a White House VIP pass.

"I said: 'Boy, I'd really like to meet Ronald Reagan,' and pretty soon, here he comes, walking right up to me," he relates. "You think you're ready, that you know what you're going to say, and then you sort of freeze: it's the President, the Commander in Chief, standing in front of you. I said, 'It's an honor, Mr. President. Thank you for taking the time out.' We chatted a moment, and he offered me some jelly beans. It was a wonderful experience."

But the most meaningful of those have occurred in nursing homes where his youthful presence and ideas have affected lives. He describes the time he asked a woman what her husband, an Alzheimer's patient, used to do, and she said he was a musician who played harmonica. Acting on a hunch, Helsing asked a staff member to purchase one.

"I put it in his hands, and he put it to his mouth and started playing," Helsing says. "They told a daughter, who hardly ever visited, and she came that night with her father's expensive harmonica. He played the most beautiful music you've ever heard. After that, the daughter came every night to hear her father play."

Helsing, who has roomed with World War I veterans, knows his circumstances are unusual. "If it wasn't for an organization like Life Care, where would someone like me be cared for," he asks.

He offers heartfelt advice to his own generation. "If you put a mother or father in a nursing home, stay in touch with them. They still have a lot of love, emotion, feelings. You can wake them up."

Gary Helsing, 49, Life Care Center of Citrus County, Lecanto, Florida

HEART IN THE CLOUDS

Galen Potter: *Aviation Pioneer*

As a master mechanic of flying machines, from trainer bombers to Air Force Ones, the cherubic-looking man helped advance the aircraft industry in war-time and peace.

In 1932, as a 19-year-old Michigan farm boy, Galen Potter drove from the heartland in a car he pieced together himself to answer his calling. He was bound for California where the aircraft industry had taken wing. Enrolling in Curtis Wright Aviation Technical Institute, he received 1,800 hours of aeronautical training and graduated in two years with a master mechanic's license.

Soon he was hired by Vultee Aircraft (it later became General Dynamics) to build the BT-13, an advanced training plane for bomber pilots. When war descended, he helped mass produce the plane that gave hands-on experience to thousands of American and allied pilots who would fly bombing missions in World War II.

At Vultee's Downey, California, plant, he played a pivotal role in launching the "Rosy the Riveter" program by hiring women to perform heretofore male-only defense-industry jobs. "He always championed women in the work place," says his daughter, Gail Bonn. "He felt if they could do the job, they should have it."

His female employees ran with the challenge, and he helped accelerate their progress. Among his methods for keeping the pace of war-time production high was putting women on roller skates to speed deliveries within the sprawling assembly plant.

His passion for planes was boundless. An excellent pilot himself, he performed aerial acrobatics in Hollywood films and made headlines in the mid 1930s by performing a double loop of the center span of the Golden Gate Bridge.

His knowledge of the BT-13 took him to Turkey in 1937 with 50 of the planes packed in crates, where he taught the Turkish air force and President Ataturk's daughter to fly them.

He met legendary aviators Amelia Earhart, Wiley Post and Howard Hughes. After the war, he managed a Los Angeles aviation company where he coordinated interior work for the private planes of such notables as Frank Sinatra and Elvis Presley.

"He never touted his association with famous people; it was just an everyday happening," says his daugh-

ter. She recalls that movie actor Robert Taylor appeared in their home one morning in fly-fishing gear as if he was a neighbor dropping by for an outing. "Dad was flying him to a lake," she says.

Renowned for his skills, he was later to coordinate interior work on three in the series of Air Force One jets that carry the President and top government officials around the world.

Through it all, he remained the unassuming farm boy who found a lofty calling and spread a gift across the skies.

Galen Potter, 86, Cottesmore of Life Care, Gig Harbor, Washington

A CHARMED EXISTENCE

Jack Johnston: *Hollywood Cameraman*

As a young man, he hopped a freighter to Tahiti and survived a shipwreck on a deserted island. In war-time, he found some of the best quarters in overseas service. In peace-time, he spent years on the set of one of America's most popular TV shows.

Wherever Jack Johnston — man of adventure and free spirit — landed, he seemed to fare well.

A third generation Los Angelene, Johnston was the grandson of Isaac Newton Johnston, who in 1909 founded the first electric irrigation pump company in California. While he adored his grandfather, the independence-loving grandson wasn't about to follow a business path.

Instead, he and a friend booked passage in 1938 on a freighter bound for Tahiti. On the return trip to California a year later, their boat was caught in a South Pacific storm and grounded on a reef. They managed to swim to a deserted island where they were rescued by a passing trawler after two weeks.

In 1941, with America on the brink of war, Johnston enlisted in the Navy. When it was learned he had dabbled in still and motion picture photography while a student at the University of Southern California, he was assigned to the Navy's photography corps. Two weeks after Pearl Harbor was bombed, Johnston was shipped to the Hawaiian Islands to begin four years of filming ship and troop movements from military reconnaissance planes.

Because Kodak operated a large film processing plant in Honolulu, Johnston and other Navy photographers received permission to live off-base, in the Hawaiian capital, so they would have immediate access to the plant. "It made the war years some of the best in my father's life," says his son, Jay.

After the war, Johnston went to Washington, D.C. to work on TV shows for the Navy, meeting stars who made promotional appearances for the service. Back in California, he gravitated to filming commercials and then began a six-year stint as one of three regular cameramen on the highly rated Mary Tyler Moore Show.

"The first day of rehearsal, we'd hear the script and walk through scenes to figure out where the three cameras should be," he explains. "Dolly positions for each shot were taped on the floor. During rehearsals, we'd fine-tune camera angles, writing notes to ourselves on each scene. When we were ready to film, communications between the three of us was unusually strong and something new. That was really interesting."

He enjoyed his association with Moore. "She was lovely, very much a lady," he says. "She had your utmost consideration in mind." Television and movie actors were generally pleasant to work with, says Johnston, who praises Moore, co-star Ed Asner and fellow cast members for their dedication to the TV series. "The amount of work it requires to learn lines and polish a performance is just brutal," he explains.

Johnston enjoyed the friendly banter on the set, done in an effort to keep cast and crew relaxed. "Oh, God, yes, there were funny times," says a man whose life seems a scrapbook of golden moments.

Jack Johnston, 84, Hallmark Manor, Federal Way, Washington

EVER READY FOR LIFE

Dorothy Giehm: Landscape Painter

Listen up, youngsters. (That's anyone under the age of 100.) Here's a Dorothy Giehm week-in-review:

Monday: Finish a landscape canvas at your Pima College painting class. Thursday: Decorate ceramics at the "Paint Yourself Silly" craft center. Sunday: Attend morning worship services at your local church and an opening-night performance of the Tucson opera. In between: Start another novel and blow out 107 candles on your birthday cake, setting off cheers and the Life Care Center of Tucson smoke alarm.

Dorothy Giehm is always drawing attention — not just for living so long but so well. Adventurous in spirit, she took up painting at 102, and it's now a passion in life. Her images of the Grand Canyon and Canada's emerald-blue Lake Louise, rendered in vibrant hues, become treasured gifts for friends. Asked why she keeps so busy a schedule, she gives a Northeasterner's no-nonsense reply: "I don't like to be idle."

She began more than a century of activity in the southern New York hamlet of Dunraven (later renamed Margaretville) where she was born in 1892, before the Spanish-American War was fought and electric lights were burning. Her father owned sawmills and resorts in the Catskill Mountains. Her grandfather invented the offset tooth that gives the saw its powerful bite.

Some of that steel passed to Dorothy. She became a teacher, working first in one-room school houses in the Catskills and Mohawk Valley. In the late 1920s, she took a post in the New Jersey public school system, then moved to Brooklyn where she taught social science to ten-year-olds for 35 years. "I

loved the fifth grade," she says, "because that's the age when kids begin to discover who they are and think for themselves."

A martinet as a teacher, Giehm mellowed with age, receiving the affectionate appellation, "Aunt Dorothy," from the many she has met in later life. Fearing she would be treated as old if people knew her real age, the active, young-looking Giehm kept her birthdays a secret until she passed 100. She agreed then to go public to show the world that age can't hold you back. Grade-school

students join her nursing-home colleagues for her annual birthday bash that draws local television crews and commendations from the mayor. The teacher in her aroused, Giehm will quiz the youngsters and looks for signs of "rascalness" in their eyes. Then she imparts words of wisdom:

"If you want to live a long full life," she tells them, "stay interested in people and what they are doing, keep active and have faith in God."

Sound advice, Aunt Dorothy, for any age.

Dorothy Giehm, 107, Life Care Center of Tucson, Arizona

BUILDING UP THE PLACE

Roger Hartwick: *Mojave Farmer*

It is a harsh place to come to, the Mojave Desert. Searing heat, boiling dust and low-growing scrub make it a land scoured of amenities. Roger Hartwick saw the rawness, and the promise, and fell in love.

His family was driven by events to Hinckley, California, a farming valley eight miles west of Barstow in the heart of the Mojave. They'd first moved from Pennsylvania, where his father was a logger, to Redlands, California, near Los Angeles, so that a sister who'd contracted tuberculosis while nursing soldiers in World War I might be helped by the air.

Then the Depression struck, and the Hartwicks pushed on to Hinckley where they bought 80 acres along the dry Mojave River (its water runs below ground) and began a dairy farm. The family sold milk to the Santa Fe Railroad, which operated a large switchyard in Barstow. "We grew alfalfa to feed the cattle and came to own as much as 1,000 acres," Hartwick recalls.

The family farm passed to him, and he and his wife, Nola, a Kansan whom he met when she visited friends in Barstow, raised turkeys and chickens (along with three children), grew vegetables and alfalfa, and tended the herd. They dug a pool in the backyard of the home he built himself

and hosted swim parties for their children and baptisms for their neighbors.

Roger Hartwick wasn't content to care only for his family. There was a community with needs. He joined the Hinckley school board and was instrumental in building a new, expanded grade school for the small farming outpost. Neighbors named the school after him.

He became a director of the 28th Agricultural District Association and a director of the San Bernardino County Fair, a post he held for 35 years. An innovator, he planted the first commercial cotton crop in the area, hoping the desert would one day be white with blooms. It didn't work, but it was worth the try.

It seems improbable the Mojave could flood, but it happens. The worst was in the 1950s when melting snow from mountains to the west engorged dry creek beds near Barstow, and the receding water claimed four feet of farming topsoil, depleting the land. To prevent a reoccurrence, he helped create and then chaired the San Bernardino County Flood Authority. Dikes and a dam were built to curtail damage from flash floods. Long after he retired from the post, he was still affectionately called "chairman of the board."

The Hartwicks were a compassionate family. Nola fed hoboes who rode the rails during the Depression. Roger served boards that improved community life. "We did everything we could for the community and its families," he says. "And I enjoyed doing it all."

Roger Hartwick, 93, Rimrock Villa
Convalescent Hospital, Barstow, CA

SOFIE'S CHOICE

Sofie Panettiere: *War Heroine*

It was at the nadir of the last century, in the heart of Nazi Germany, that Sofie Panettiere kept a secret that spared a family's life, even as she risked her own.

She was barely 30 years old when Hitler's war machine rolled across Europe. Panettiere worked in Berlin for a man whose company operated plants in Germany and abroad. He was a Lutheran, but a grandparent of his had been Jewish. "To the Nazis," says Panettiere, "that made him Jewish." And a trace of Jewish blood could doom a family to confiscation of property, deportation and death.

The business owner instinctively trusted his young employee. She was a strong-willed, spirited person. Born in Stuttgart, she had lost her father when she was a child, and her mother had married a man who was a director of the Bank of Germany. A friend of her stepfather's, who was a Jew, was shot by the Nazis during their rise to power.

"We hated Hitler; we knew he was a madman," says Panettiere, who refused any affiliation with the Nazis. "A Jewish friend asked me once if I was a member of the Nazi Party," she says. "I said, 'No!' He laughed and said to a friend: 'Sofie, she does what she wants.'"

Life during the war was harrowing, but Panettiere knew little of fear. She used forged papers to move about the country. Once, during a parade led by Hitler through the streets of Nuremberg, she pretended to faint so she would be picked up and carried across the lines without having to wait for the procession to pass.

Panettiere describes her boss as a "very kind and considerate man" who was obviously fearful for the family secret. He confided in Panettiere and gave her authority to sign company documents and make decisions should he be arrested. "He knew if he was discovered by the Nazis, neither his wife's signature nor that of other family members would be any good," she says.

For three years, Panettiere helped him run his business and kept his secret. Eventually, though, it was learned. The Gestapo burst into his office one day and threw him in a chair. "We should arrest the whole office," they threatened, before carting him alone off to jail. Having already fled to Switzerland, his wife was spared imprisonment. The war, however, was in its final months, and the man soon was freed, going on to become a member of the Geneva Conference.

In the aftermath of Germany's defeat, Panettiere battled for human concerns. She petitioned the American commander of the occupying force near her hometown of Stuttgart to keep factories open so people would have work and could survive. "He kept dismissing me, and I kept coming back," she says of her stubborn determination. "Finally, I convinced him."

She managed to obtain papers to leave Germany in January 1947 and fly to America. "When I got to New York City, they locked me up. 'That Nazi,' they said, 'what are we going to do with her.' My fiancee (the same American commander who had dismissed her) got me out of jail. The first thing we did was get married."

As Sofie had protected others, now she was safe.

Sofie Panettiere, 87, Life Care Center of Ocala, Florida

AN EYE FOR DRAMA

Jim Petrie: Documentary Filmmaker

Two men shout instructions while peering in your eyes. A siren blares. It dies, and a wedge of sky appears, replaced by streaming overhead lights. Two large doors swing open, and the frantic movement stops. You stare into a bank of round, white lights. A cupped mask slowly descends, growing larger as it fills your frame of view, and everything goes black.

Welcome to Jim Petrie's dramatic world. He shot this harrowing scene lying on his back on a rolling gurney with a 16-millemeter camera pointed upward. He chose a patient's perspective to take you on a ride, from an ambulance through an emergency department to an operating room. He wanted you to feel in your bones the blessing of a hospital's emergency service. His goal was to win your support for the facility.

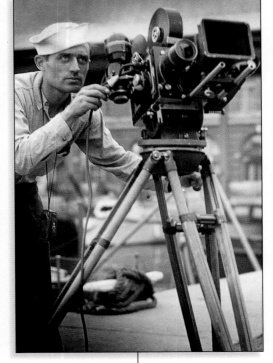

Petrie spent a career in filmmaking, first to entertain Americans on the widest screens, then to move them to good works through short, highly-charged productions. Along the way, he won awards, worked with industry legends, and generated contributions for social agencies.

The Boston native attended the city's School of the Museum of Fine Arts and studied design in Paris. When World War II broke out, his visual talents found another use. After attending the Navy's motion picture school, he filmed plastic models of Japanese terrain to orient American pilots and bombardiers flying missions over that country. Japan surrendered, however, before the films were used.

After the war, he set his sights on big-studio movie-making. Hired as a New England location scout by director Louis De Rochemont, he found the settings for a series of 1950s films that included "Lost Boundaries," "Whistle at Eaton Falls," "Walk East on Beacon" and "Windjammer."

He also scouted Western locations for the 1955 giant-screen production, "Cinerama Holiday," and found the starring couple for the film. "That was a fun job," says Petrie, who attended the movie's debut at The Roxie in New York City.

He traded the flashing marquis for a small film-production company that he opened with two partners on New York's Times Square. "When you did everything yourself, as we did, it was more creative," he says. An early project was a film for the Greater New York Fund, which supported the work of social service agencies in New York City, Southern Connecticut and Northern New Jersey.

So successful was Petrie's film in raising money for the non-profit Fund that the project became an annual assignment. "It took us a whole year to produce a film that was ten minutes long," he says. "We had a wonderful script writer from the *New York Daily News*, and our narrators included Gregory Peck, Robert Taylor and Orson Wells."

An innovator of visual techniques, Jim Petrie received filmmaking recognition. His greatest achievement, though, came in making his audiences care.

Jim Petrie, 86, Life Care Center of Nashoba Valley, Littleton, Massachusetts

TO SMITHFIELD, WITH LOVE

Margaret Crepeau: Town Clerk

For almost 50 years, one couldn't mark a passage of life in the small town of Smithfield, Rhode Island — not a birth or a marriage or a death — without Margaret Crepeau's official, and affectionate, blessing.

As town clerk, she was keeper of its citizens' records, from the cradle to the grave. "When you're born," she explains, "your birth certificate is recorded in the town clerk's office and when you die, we issue the burial permit." In all things governing community life, from public ordinances to personal wills, she was involved.

This was more than a job for Crepeau. Her roots were in Smithfield, where her father and his mother were born and where she, herself, lived for 75 years. "I cried with every burial permit I issued," she says, "because I knew the people."

Her devotion to a town that became her extended family began at age 17 when the town clerk at the time inquired of her father: "I hear your Margaret graduated from high school. How would she like to work for me?"

Truth be told, Crepeau wanted to be a teacher, but she was the middle of 11 children in her family, and there wasn't money for college. She took the job, starting as a typist, and becoming in turn assistant and deputy town clerk. In 1948, she won election as the first female town clerk in Rhode Island history and, after repeated re-election victories, was granted life tenure in the post.

It wasn't breaking barriers but touching lives that gave Crepeau her sense of purpose. She was caring for people in their moments of joy and grief, and if it required the 70-hour work week she averaged, so be it.

It was no surprise that the community inducted her into its Hall of Fame. The mayor, the district congressman and 100 citizens gathered one evening to bestow the honor. Such impressive professional achievements as reviving the Rhode Island Town and City Clerk's Association, which she served as president, were cited, but it was her countless acts of kindness that attendees cherished recounting.

"I feel I made a great many friends, and they still come from out of the blue to visit. I get some of the same recognition as a teacher," Crepeau says fondly.

Coming from a large family, Crepeau expected she and her husband, Bob, would raise children of their own, but several miscarriages and a failed adoption intervened. The void was filled with good works for a town. "Smithfield was like family," she says. "They were my children."

Margaret Crepeau, 88, Cherry Hill Manor Nursing Home, Johnston, Rhode Island

ROOTING FOR THE EARTH

Charles Birch: *Environmental Prophet*

Charles Birch launched his mission to save the planet modestly enough, collecting 20 sprouting acorns in a Ziploc bag. But his plan was far-reaching: "If we can get every family to double the growth of trees on their property and if we can create vast forests in sparsely settled regions of the globe," he declares, "we can replenish atmospheric oxygen and reverse the depletion of the ozone layer."

So one September, in his mid-80s, Charles Birch planted the sprouting acorns on a gently sloping bank of his Massachusetts home at Life Care Center of Plymouth. As the seedlings took root, he collected more acorns and nurtured them in small pots that lined the sill of the large picture window in his room.

Meanwhile, he spread his gospel on the world-wide Internet. Using the moniker, OZONECHARL, he dispensed scientific data on warming trends, decried the fouling of the planet by pollution and explained the cost it will exact on future generations. He also described his solution, which included turning arid regions of the globe into giant, irrigated tree farms.

Why devote so much energy so late in life to a monumental (some might say quixotic) goal? "I have children and grandchildren," he declares, "and I feel responsible for what's taking place."

His passion for the natural world came naturally enough, from outdoor-loving parents who took their children on vacations to the mountains and ponds of Vermont. "Even as a youngster, I liked to study the leaves; I found them fascinating," he says.

He gravitated to the outdoors in adult ventures which included a ski area built from scratch in Duchess County, New York. He cleared slopes and trails himself, constructed the lodge, offered the novelty of outdoor music to ski by, and became a pioneer in making snow.

His interest in the environment propelled him briefly into the national spotlight when, in the late 1980s, ABC's "Good Morning, America" interviewed him from his Pennsylvania home about his concept for converting underground coal fires into harnessable, energy. Perhaps, because the idea seemed too simple and cheap, it was never tried.

Other environmental battles were won. When a company wanted to locate a dump he believed toxic in his town, he was up in arms, threatening to seek the help of local officials, state representatives and federal regulators. The developer scuttled the plan.

According to his daughter, Cathryn Condron, Birch has always been an impassioned advocate for just causes. "He always got involved wherever he went," she says. "One time a child was lost in the Adirondacks. Dad got in his car and drove four hours to join the search. He always does what he can to help. He always does what he thinks is right."

Charles Birch, 87, Life Care Center of Plymouth, MA

SHE SHALL OVERCOME

Annie Desilets: Working Mother

Annie Dunford Desilets was almost buried before she had a chance to live.

The Rhode Island undertaker who placed her infant body in a wicker basket after she'd been crushed by the wheel of a trolley on Sharkstone Avenue in Providence in 1910 thought she was surely dead. On his way to the mortuary, an Irish woman, who saw a limb move in the basket, called out: "Now what's the matter with you? That baby's alive!"

Her left heel severed, her left hip crushed and her head gashed open, the 18-month-old underwent emergency surgery. As she slowly regained consciousness, doctors feared she'd be mentally and physically impaired for life. To test her faculties, they had her grandmother bring a doll dressed in pink to the hospital room and offer it to the child. "I don't want *that* doll," remonstrated Annie, who possessed a spunky, tomboyish nature. "I want a blue one."

One trial down in the spirited life of Annie Desilets; more to come. She hobbled through childhood on crutches, which she despised. "My grandmother said I couldn't walk without them, but I wanted to be like the other kids," she recalls. So she hid the crutches, claiming they were lost, and ran after her friends "hippety-hoppety," with one leg shorter than the other."

When she was 13, her father abandoned his wife and four children. To help the impoverished family survive, Desilets was hired out to a laundry, working 12 hours a day for $7 a week and getting what schooling she could at night. Because her employment violated child labor laws, the laundry owners hid her in a bathroom whenever state inspectors paid a visit.

Neither injury nor poverty nor lack of schooling could stop Annie Desilets. Despite a deformed hip and leg, she grew into an attractive woman whose strawberry-blonde hair and flashing green eyes helped her capture the Miss Olneyville Square title in Providence in her late teens. "They were going to give me a beautiful gown as a prize, but where the heck was I going to wear it," she says. "I took the money, instead."

She married her husband, Paul, in 1929. Doctors doubted she could have children because of residual scar tissue, but after losing her first child a few hours after birth, she delivered two healthy children: Anne and Paul, Jr. There have grown to be four generations of Anne's in the family, all named for the feisty matriarch.

While she never graduated from high school, she was a voracious reader and self-taught student. After holding a "Rosy the Riveter" defense plant job during the Second World War, she worked for 25 years as an inspector in a General Electric manufacturing plant. Fiercely independent, she took pride in being able to help support her family.

It came as no surprise to the family that a day after total hip replacement surgery at the age of 89, she was walking and then singing during the painful rehabilitation therapy.

"My mother is a remarkable woman," says her daughter, Anne Oliver. "When we were growing up, she would wake up singing each morning. Despite the problems she faced, I never heard her complain. She felt you have to go on living. Besides, as she'd always tell us: 'Life is sweet.'"

Annie Desilets, 90, Life Care Center of Paradise Valley, Phoenix, Arizona

TOUGH — WITH WORDS

Pete Cassler: *Cowboy Poet*

He broke wild horses and drilled wildcat wells, ran a 30,000-acre ranch, patrolled the U.S. border on horseback (where he shot and killed a smuggler in self defense), and carried winter provisions by mule train to foresters working knee-deep in snow in the high Sierra mountains.

Pete Cassler's powerful hands are veined from hard work, and his eyes can still contract to the hard glint that stopped men bent on fighting him dead in their tracks.

What you wouldn't expect in Cassler is the soul of a poet. Yet, he's labored years to perfect an eight-line poem and written verse published in an anthology by the National Library of Poetry. With the power of simple words, he captures in "Aspen" the character of the western tree he loves:

"The Aspen are like children/ Dancing in their dreams,/ All along the hillside/ And on the banks of streams./ The pines, they are like dowagers/ Nodding in the wind,/ Predicting that these children/ Will come to no good end."

Cassler began a footloose journey through life when he traveled as a young man from his native Missouri to New Mexico, where he spent eight years managing a ranch in the shadows of the Sacramento Mountains. Of all the jobs he worked, ranching was the best suited to his independent spirit.

"You got on your horse each morning, and no one had to tell you what to do," he says. "There was no boss standing over your shoulder. It was all your responsibility. And if you made a mistake, you didn't make it twice."

Worst of the jobs was patrolling the Mexican border in a desolate corner of Arizona and New Mexico. His purpose was to intercept contraband drugs, gold and money, pitting him against desperate men. "I got shot at several times and a knife stuck in me once. It wasn't good," he says. "I knew sooner or later they'd kill me."

So he drilled oil wells, losing a summer's wage when one came up dry ("But what if we'd hit something," he says, relishing the thought), played banjo for barn dances and second base for a semi-pro team, and found his way to California, where he carried supplies by mule train to Forest Service camps in the high mountain passes and cooked surpassingly light sourdough biscuits for the men.

His formal schooling ended in the tenth grade, but he attracted educated, well-read friends, for he was a lover of books and a student of life. "If I hadn't read and hadn't traveled, I wouldn't be intelligent," he says. "But I learned from every place I went."

And he wrote verse along the way. In "Quakie," a title based on the cowboy name for the Aspen, he has the tree describe the human yearning to return to your native place:

"When I was a little tree/Tall enough to sway/They dug me up with some earth/And took me far away. Now I am an old "Quakie"/At a place they call their home/Longing for the mountains/And the trees they left alone."

Pete Cassler, 88, Life Care Center of Evergreen, Colorado

"The sun setting is no less beautiful than the sun rising."

Japanese proverb